T4-APV-100

THE MESSIAH HAS COME

Published by:
Nirman Publisher
P. O. Box 55201
Bridgeport, CT 06610

THE

MESSIAH

HAS

COME

by
Shantilal Kapadia

NIRMAN PUBLISHER

CONTENTS

1	Prophecy	1
2	Sign of New Times	14
3	Why Is He Born In India	20
4	Childhood	36
5	First Call of Gurudev	48
6	A Soldier For Independence	67
7	The Second Phase of Journey	71
8	In Mathura	80
9	The Great Gayatri Mantra	87
10	New Age Force	103
11	Yagna	112
12	Third Pilgrimage to the Himalayas	115
13	Miracle	120
14	Shanti Kunj	131
15	The Fourth and Final Direction	145
16	Astral Body	150
17	The Prediction	159
18	Two Words	166

NOTES

The following chapters and parts of chapters are taken directly from books written by Shree Ram Sharma Acharya, published by Yug Nirman Yojna of Mathura and Brahmavarchash of Hardwar. To enhance clarity for western readers, some changes were made to the translation.

Chapter 5, "First Call of Gurudev" from the book, *My Will and My Heritage*, written by Shree Ram Sharma Acharya.

Chapter 7, "The Second Phase of Journey and Assessment of the Field of Work", written by Shree Ram Sharma Acharya.

Chapter 10, "The New Age Force", written by Shree Ram Sharma Acharya.

Chapter 12, "Third Pilgrimage to the Himalayas-- Sowing of the Seeds of Rushi Tradition", written by Shree Ram Sharma Acharya.

Chapter 15, "The Fourth and Final Direction", written by Shree Ram Sharma Acharya.

In Chapter 16, "Transformation of the Physical into Astral: Sookshmikaran" in brief, from the book, *My Will and My Heritage*, written by Shree Ram Sharma Acharya.

In Chapter 17, "My prophecy is that there will not be destruction but creation", written by Shree Ram Sharma Acharya.

PREFACE

This book is the product of faith in God, hope for the future and the love of many people.

Most especially, I heartily thank His Holiness P.P. Gurudev Shree Ram Sharma Acharya, Brahmavarchash and Yug Nirman Yogja who gave their permission for me to reprint their articles. I also heartily thank poonjya Shree Shastriji, Nityanand Patel and others for their cooperation.

Very special thanks to my son Prakash, his wife Meenaxi and her brother Bharat for their constant help in translating and critiquing. Thanks also to Edward Hopkins, James Bair, Debbie Jenestreet, Ben Carrara and to Stephen Ellerin for his editorial assistance.

OAM SHANTIHI, SHANTIHI, SHANTIHI.

Let there Be Peace, Peace, Peace!

POO. SHREE RAM SHARMA ACHARYA

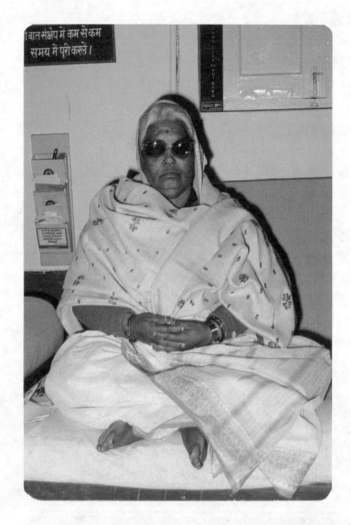

SHREE BHAGWATIDEVI SHARMA

Chapter 1

Prophecy

The Universe has given birth to many prophets. These people use in born, Divine powers to foresee future events. When they speak, people listen; most people do believe.

Jesus said that he would return with all power and glory. Jesus said,

"I saw one approaching, like a Son of Man, upon the Clouds of Heaven. When He reached the ancient one and was presented before him, He received dominion and glory. All peple shall come to serve Him. His dominion is everlasting and shall endure forever". (Daniel 7:13-14).

The *Clouds of Heaven* means a specific place. Rushis and Munis (Hindu titles for ancient sages; each title indicates the degree of Divine Power achieved) and Saints, all of whom were born thousands of years ago, live today in the Himalayas. It is said that, in the old days, Sages lived in the region between Rushikesh and Gomukh and that the region above Gomukh was abode of Gods--Clouds of Heaven. People believe that Gods live in Heaven. Hindus believed that the upper part of the Himalayas is the *Clouds of Heaven*. Many epics tell of noble journeys to

SHREE SARVESHWARANANDJI
(DADA GURUDEV)

Heaven. The *Mahabharat* tells that when the Pandave (five sons of the king, Padav) wanted to go to Heaven, they climbed the Himalaya. Maganath, son of King Rawan, defeated King Indra of Heaven. These feats are typical of many heroes of Indian history. So *Clouds of Heaven* is the upper part of the Himalayas.

When he reached the ancient one and was presented before him . . . : Shree Ram Sharma was called four times by Swami Sarveshwaranandji, who lives on Mahendragiri Mountain in the Himalayas at a height of 22,000 feet. Shree Ram brought a camera to take a picture of Swami Sarveshwaranandji. He took two pictures. Today, when asked about the age of his "Gurudev", Shree Ram replies, "If I tell people that he is more than 600 years old, they would ask for a medical check-up." So he simply calls Swami Sarveshwaranandji "old". However, Shree Ram Sharma believes that Swami Sarveshwaranandji is more than 600 years old.

According to the epic *Kalkipuran*, the Swami Sarveshwaranandji is the Bhagwan (God) Parshuram. Bhagwan Parshuram was the sixth Incarnation of the Ten Main Incarnations of the Divine Soul, according to Hindu belief. Born in the Sat Yug, a period spanning about 4,000 years, Bhagwan Parshuram showed up at the wedding of Lord Shree Ram, who was the Divine Soul's seventh Incarnation, born during the Treta Yug, a period spanning the following 3,000 years, as related in the historical book, *Ramayan*. Bhagwan Shree Parshuram taught the science of archery to Karna, a son of King Pandev, in the Dwapar Yug, the third period, which lasted 2,000 years. Today, we are at the end of the Kali Yug, a

THE BRAHMAVARCHAS RESEARCH CENTER

period of 1,000 years. Simple addition, then, makes
Swami Sarveshwaranandji, the Gurudev of Shree
Ram Sharma Acharya, more than 7,000 years old. The
devout practitioner of Yoga can achieve whatever he
wishes. Swami Yoganand, founder of The Self-
Realization Fellowship, wrote in his book *An
Autobiography of a Yogi* that he met "Avatari Baba,"
who is deathless.

It is stated in Urdu (Muslim-language) literature
written in the Hijari year 1289 (1569 A.D.) that "150
years before, in Hardwar, Shree Gulhasanshah met
with Swami Shavanath. At the same time, he met with
a saint of the Himalayas who is more than 400 years
old. He dwells on the Mahendragiri Mountain at a
height of 22,000 feet. Although the snow covers this
spot all year long, he lives there without shoes or even
clothes. According to Swami Golalishah, the Gurudev
of Gulhasanshah, he is Swami Sarveshwaranandji.
Swami Golalishah said that, every 90 years, Swami
Sarveshwaranandji transforms himself into a boy of
twelve.

When Shree Ram reached the mountain
dwelling, Swami Sarveshwaranandji presented him to
many ancient Rushis, Munis, and Saints. Madame
Blavatsky[1] described these Rushis and Munis as

---

[1]Madame Helena Petrovna Blavatsky (1831-91), co-
founder of the Theosophical Society, advocated a universal
brotherhood of mankind. She postulated the existence of
Rushis, Munis, and sages of superhuman knowledge who
lived in the Himalayas. She said that these Rushis, Munis,
and sages had given her the power to disclose some of their
secret knowledge. She brought to the West a knowledge of
Yoga, meditation, reincarnation, and vegetarianism.

"invisible helpers" and as "a Government for the welfare of human beings." These ancient Rushis and Munis assigned Shree Ram a task--to work every day for the welfare of all people of the world, which will give him dominion, glory, and everlasting kingship, which all people will acknowledge in the near future.

To justify the sages in the Himalayas, Jesus repeatedly said,

> *"The kingdom and power and greatness of*
> *the Kingdom under the whole Heaven may*
> *be given to people of the saints of the Most*
> *High; Whose Kingdom is an everlasting*
> *Kingdom, and all kings shall serve Him,*
> *and shall obey Him." (Daniel 7:27).*

The New Testament does not tell what Jesus Christ did for twelve years of his life. Mr. N.A. Notovich, in his book *Unknown Life of Jesus Christ*, and Mr. Levi, in his book, *The Aquarian Gospel of Jesus the Christ*, say that Jesus travelled to India and stayed with Brahmins and Buddhists for many years. There he learned Sanskrit. This period of training made a great impression on Jesus and His teachings Mr. Notovich asserts. Indeed, many scholars from various countries have argued that much of Christian theology derives from Buddhist thought. Swami Yogananda said in his book *Man's Eternal Quest* that the many similarities between Jesus' teachings and those of yoga strongly support records known in India. He believed that Jesus and Krishna were one, and so do I. The movie named "The History of Jesus Christ" documented that Jesus dwelt in India during these twelve years. He went to the Himalayas for penance; while there He must have achieved Divine power.

Why did Jesus Christ go there? Since the dawn of history, Rushis, Munis, and Saints have done penance on Himalayas. It is told in the ancient Indian epic, *Ramayan*, that Lord Shree Ram went to Dev-prayag in the Himalayas for penance. A few years ago, the famous saint, Anand Swami of Arya Samaj, went for penance in the Himalayas. The Divine atmosphere seems richer in the Himalayas, the highest mountain range on Earth. It has been clearly stated in Isaiah 2:2 that:

"in the last days the mountain of the Lord's House shall be established on the <u>highest mountain</u> raised above the hills."

"In the last days . . . " represents the last days of this era. Prophets of the world have foretold that 2000 A.D. will user in a new era. The *highest mountains* in the world lie in the Himalayas. The "Lord's House" is the place of the Rushi and Munis who are so concerned with the welfare of mankind.

People lost in the Himalayas credit their lives to help from these Rushis and Saints. The newspaper *Sandesh*, of Ahmedabad, India, published an account by a holy man who went in search of such Rushis and Saints, but sought in vain and lost his way. After a whole day's search, suddenly he saw the glow of a lantern streaming from the window of a small cottage. He made his way to the entrance of the cottage and saw one saint inside. He bowed down and received the Saint's blessing. The saint asked if he was hungry and asked what he should like to eat. The man stated his preference, and the Saint went to the back of the cottage and brought the requested food in less than one minute. After eating, the seeker asked the Saint for directions back to his hotel. At the Saint's command, the traveller closed his eyes, and found himself instantly back in his room.

In the Fifth Chapter of his book *Present and Future Prophecies*, Dr. E. Stanton interprets the Bible to mean that the rider sitting on the white horse gradually opened seven gold coins and, within a few moments, changed the thinking of the people there. Without spilling a drop of blood, he improved everyone's life and drove the Satanic influence from the people. In this, he concurs with the Reverend Mr. Baxter who, citing Chapter Six of Revelation, writes that a man on a white horse with a sword in his hand is born: White symbolizes knowledge; "A sword in his hand" means a person with Divine Knowledge and Divine Power is born who will bring revolutionary change to the world and will turn the eyes of all people to God. He will appear amidst suffering, when the God of Death will stop the population explosion with disease and natural calamities. The Divine One will bring peace, humanity, and brotherhood among all people.

These two interpretations invite comparison between Kalkipuran and Christianity. In Kalkipuran, white symbolizes knowledge and the sword signifies the removal of atheism through the medium of Intelligence. This revolution in thought will come from all four directions so fast that the Heavenly Kingdom of Peace will be established before some people know that the revolution is underway, as with current changes in Eastern Europe, Russia, South Africa, and other countries.

Daniel 2:44 states, *"The Kingdom of the Almighty will be in the form of Power."* His theosophy will establish a universal theocracy.

The Kalkipuran, an Indian epic that deals with life and reincarnation, although written thousands of years ago, backs the statements of Rev. Baxter. It says that He shall have the "sign of the Second Day of the New Moon," a sign similar to the English letter "v", on his forehead, between his eyebrows. (See the picture of Shree Ram.) I have seen the predicted birthmark on Shree Ram's forehead. Shree Ram's caste matches the prediction in the Kalkipuran text; he has three brothers, as predicted; he was born near Mathura, as promised; and he has moved north of Mathura, leaving Suryaketu in charge of his administration, as foretold in the Kalkipuran.

Many whose prophecies have proven true, including Nostradamus; Jules Verne of France; Prof. Harar of Israel; the German philosopher, Schopenhauer; Mother Shrimpton from the United Kingdom; Mrs. Jean Dixon; Mr. Edgar Cayce; Mr. M.W. Armstrong, the president of the Worldwide Church of God and editor of the magazine *Plain Truth*; prophet and astrologer, Mr. Anderson; Mr. George Bavera from Miser; the well-known Muslim scholar, Saiyed Katub; the editor of *Healing Life*, Mr. John Mullard; from Norway, Swami Anand; astrologer Mr. Charles Clark; Mr. Gerard Chrise of Holland; Roma Rola, astrologer; Madam Boriska Silviger from Hungary; Prof. Cheiro; and, from India, Maharsi Arvindo Ghosh, Swami Vivekanand, Raman Swami Ayaark, Swami Ashminand, Mr. Rajnaran Sarshastri, Mr. Kedardat Joshi, Swami

Jagadishanandji, Mr. Shastri Chulait, and others have said, in essence, that a messenger [Author's Note: the English word "angel" comes from the Greek word for "messenger"] has been born near Mathura, in India. He will participate in the fight for independence of India. His organization will be run by a married couple. His wife will look after its administration. This divine man will have the sign of the second-day moon on his forehead. He will perform miracles, and science will blaze the new path to religion. His organization, formed for religious uplift and universal welfare, will coincide with independence for India. In a short span of time, he will attract a large number of followers from all states. Although a man born to wealth and property, he will lead a simple life, and his wealth will be used for social welfare. People who go to him with their suffering and sorrow will find their problems vanish. With his power, he will fill the hearts of people with joy and happiness. The prophets saw visions of people chanting, putting objects into a holy fire--like the traditional Hindu ceremony of Yagna. Wearing only simple cloth, shoes made from cloth, and white hair on his head, he will be proven the most powerful man in history.

His systematically-written literature of custom and manner will be not only believed by the world, but also worshiped like the Gita and the Bible. The revolution will begin in his country and will spread throughout the world. India will be reborn as a great nation, bestowed with Almighty power, and western countries will start to adopt Indian culture--dress, food, social life, and also religion. India will be the trailblazer in new fields of research of the new sciences. The politicians of all countries will be forged into one political administration and the United Nations will move to India. A new religious revolution will arise which will reveal the secrets of God and god-consciousness. This will come to pass by the end of the year of 2000 A.D. Thereafter, the people of the world will know and share universal brotherhood, love, humanity, peace, joy, and happiness.

It is clearly stated in Matthew that the Reincarnation will come from the East, *"For as the light comes forth from the East and shines even to the West so will the coming of the Son be."* (Matthew 24:27). "Light comes forth from the East" means that the Incarnation Person will come from a country to the east of Israel, where Jesus lived and the Bible was written. Some prophets of the world have recently stated that the Person of the Incarnation has been born in India.

Nostradamus predicted, in Century V, Quatrain 53, that the Messiah will come and will achieve his power through the sun, in accord with Venus. Here "Venus" stands for the Vedic religion. He further predicted that neither "the one" religion, Christianity, nor "the other", Islam, would understand the power of the sun. Tradition links the Hindu (Vedic) goddess Gayatri with the sun, and the Gayatri spell works through the sun. Shree Ram Sharma achieved Divine Power from Gayatri's mantra through the sun. So Nostradamus' Venus stands for the Vedic (Hindu) religion. Neither Christianity nor Islam have understood the power of the sun. Eventually the Vaidyk (Vedic) religion will rule the world.

Nostradamus further said His life and work will be according to the prophecy. Shree Ram will fulfill these prophecies. In fact, if one studies all the major prophecies of the world, one will find that they match the life of Shree Ram Sharma Acharya.

Nostradamus stated in another quatrain that religious thoughts will flow from the ancient civilization [i.e., country] surrounded by water on three sides. India is surrounded by water on three sides. These thoughts will lead the world away from the road of destruction to the way of prosperity and success and will confirm the advent of the True Age.

In 1939, religious leaders from all of North India held a conference in anticipation of the imminent Incarnation. They held a long debate about incarnation in that conference and set down their revelations in a book. In brief, they agreed that this Divine Man will have the sign of the "second day moon" on his forehead between his eyebrows. He will be wearing typical Indian outer garments. His nature will be as soft as the lotus and as brave as a warrior. He will be a master of the Vedas, of scripture, and of science. The number "24" will be very prominent in his life. The Mantra he will recite will contain 24 syllables. He will do penance for 24 years and will do "devotion" of 2.4 million spells each year and his followers will do 24 million more spells (mantras) each year to charge the world's atmosphere with spirituality and user in the Age of Harmony. He will arrange 2400 celebrations of the Yagna ceremony. People will believe in him and he will "show them the secret of religion and soul."

Many well-known thinkers, astrologers, prophets of the world concur that the Age of Revolution is at hand, and that the years from 1989 to 2000 A.D. shall be the Age of Transition from the old era to the new.

Looking at the world as it stands today, one could lose faith in the power of these prophecies; however what God intends shall come to be, and man cannot prevent it. What we see around us today may pass away. Tomorrow, moral strength may prevail over temporal armies, and the power of the Divine Soul will strengthen us. Mankind will experience the Power of the Word for the first time. Already we begin to see the results, as the winds of change sweep across Eastern Europe, South Africa, and other countries.

To create this revolutionary change, 2.4 million devotees of Shree Ram have, for the last few years, recited daily the Gayatri Mantra. The power that they create will bolster his power. This power will also raise the divine soul of the Indian people and will both solve their temporal problems and give other countries the power to improve their own welfare and attain prosperity through the Gayatri Mantra.

Today, India's political and economic position is not good. However, in the near future it will become stronger. It is said in the Bible, *"The kingdom and power and greatness of the Kingdom, under the whole Heaven, may be given to the people of the saints of the Most High; whose Kingdom is an everlasting Kingdom, and all kings shall serve Him, and shall obey Him"* (Daniel 7:27). India will find divine inspiration in God, whose power will be superior to the power of arms and ammunition and money.

If one reviews all the prophecies impartially and compares them to Shree Ram Sharma, one can conclude that the Incarnation has arrived in India, and that he has started his work with six bodies, one physical and five astral bodies, for universal welfare and prosperity.

Shree Ram once asked Dada Gurudev (Swami Sayveshwaranandaji) why, when most people are not born with divine powers, Madam Blavatsky was not only born with divine powers but even made contact with the ancient sages who live in the Himalayas.

"That was our gift to her," Dada Gurudev replied. "The sages wanted the world to know that they still thrive there."

So I believe that it is justifiable that the Second Coming is here. Jesus said, in the Bible, *"When he reached the ancient one and presented before him"* (Daniel 7:13). In the past, nobody was presented to the ancient sage, nor will anyone in the future. Only being born a Son of God, the Messiah, Shree Ram Sharma, was presented to the ancient sages. To justify and witness the above Gospel, Jesus said, *"And this Gospel of the Kingdom shall be preached in the whole world, for a witness to all nations and then will come the end"* (Matthew 24:14). Shree Ram Sharma's Gospel shall be preached throughout the world.

Jesus said further to support the prophecy, *"Heaven and earth will pass away, but my words will not pass away"* (Matthew 24:35). Shree Ram Sharma is the Messiah. There will be no anti-Christ; the anti-Christ is the present age.

The 21st Century will bring with it a prosperous future where everyone will live peacefully and happily.

Christians wait for the Person of the Second Coming; Jews and devotees of Jehovah's Witness are waiting for the Person of the First Incarnation. In my opinion, Shree Ram Sharma is the Incarnation.

The Sun is the Earth's ultimate source of energy. The sun cannot hide itself; its power shines forth. In the same way, Shree Ram Sharma's work in the next decade will prove that He is the (Re-)Incarnation.

Chapter 2

Signs of New Times

Not only astrologers of more modern times, but prophets of old, and, before even them, the sacred books of all great religions have talked about times and events to come. Long before modern technology spewed out texts on high speed presses, holy prophets turned inward, and upward, to gather knowledge of the Divine and to distill their revelations into the sacred scriptures--the Hindu *Bhagwat* and *Ramayan*, the *Koran*, and the Holy Bible, passed on from well-trained mind to well-trained mind until set down in print and turned into the modern versions that we read today.

The essence of each of these works is similar. When the source of each work is the Source of the Universe, how can the written messages differ? Yet, somehow, the languages of the Holy books differ.

Come, let us look into the books of the Hindu religion, and see what the *Bhagwat* reveals:

The *Kali Yug*, it tells us, the Present Era, draws to a close. The present century has been an era of transition.

Many who tally the Ages of the World count them according to their own interpretations. Perhaps those who place the end of this era thousands of years ahead unintentionally mislead their followers. Hear, instead, what the famous Saints of India say.

Saint Surdas wrote,

Mana loh Dhiraj Kiyu Na Dhare. Jug Jug
Pragat Bhayo Re;
Ek Hajar Navso Ke upper Adbhut job pare,

meaning, "Why doesn't the mind of the people wait for He who comes in every age to show the way to destroy sinners. The surprising time of the Sat Yug, the age of truth, is just beyond the year nineteen hundred."

The famous Saint Ramdev Pir said,

Sauvat vishama Dharam Thapase Hareashe
Kshatri bhupar.
Nas Pamase sarve Droho, Desdrohine kashlo
Apar,

which means, "religion will establish in sauvat, the Twentieth Century of the era that began, by Hindu reckoning, in 56 B.C. Then there will be no more crime and traitors will suffer defeat."

In addition to religious leaders, modern psychics like Jean Dixon, Arvind Ghose, and Professor Harrar Anand Swamy, among others, have predicted that the Twenty-First Century will usher in an era of peace, love, and happiness.

The scholar and freedom fighter, Shree Lokmanya Tilak, in his book *Gita Rahaysa (Secret)*, describes the Indian way of reckoning the ages. In short, he argues that one terrestrial day equals one day of God. Therefore, 360 of our years make up one Divine year. Extending his calculations produces the following tally of Ages:

1. The Sat Yug (Age of Truth)   4000 years
        Closing Transition Period   400 years
        Opening Transition Period   400 years
2. The Tretayug (Second Age)   3000 years
        Closing Transition Period   300 years
        Opening Transition Period   300 years
3. The Dwaparyug (Third Age)   2000 years
        Closing Transition Period   200 years
        Opening Transition Period   200 years
4. The Kaliyug (Fourth Age)   1000 years
        Closing Transition Period   100 years
        Opening Transition Period   100 years

Adding the total of the transitional periods to the sum of the Ages produces 12,000 years of the Sankhaya (one of the six systems of Vedic philosophy). Accordingly, Shree Lokmanya concluded that the current century is the transitional period ending the last age.

The *Manu Smruti* (1/67-69) computes the age differently:

1. The Sat Yug Period   4800 years
2. The Tretayug Period   3600 years
3. The Dwaparyug Period   2400 years
4. The Kaliyug (Fourth Age)   1200 years

This reckoning matches that in the third chapter of the *Shrimad Bhagwat* (3:1:19).

The Van Parva of the *Mahbharat* warns that, as one age ends and the next begins, the collision of dominant themes brings inevitable unrest, even destruction. The *Mahbharat* goes on to state that when the sun, the moon, the planet Jupiter and the Pushya

Nakshatra (a star) enter the same House of the Zodiac, they signal the start of the Sat Yug Period, the Age of Truth, when miraculous events will bring the blossoming of peace, prosperity, love, and universal happiness.

This celestial conjunction occurred a few years ago. The horrors of world-scale war, major earthquakes, natural disasters and social unrest will follow.

Only as this final decade of the 1900's dawns can the rest of us see the light of hope, as changes begin to sweep Europe and South Africa.

The ancient Hindu scripture, the *Bhagwat*, describes the time from the arrival of Lord Krishna, over 3,000 years ago, through the end of this, the Kaliyug Period. All of these prophecies have come true. For example, Chapter 12 of the *Shrimad Bhagwat* predicts both the rule of India by one of the Mourya Kings, which came to pass with the reign of Mohanand, early in this century; and India's rule by a foreign people during the middle of the Fourth Age, which occurred about the year 1200 A.D., when Moslem tribes began to conquer India; and assaults of Yavan, an increase in anti-cultural behavior in day-to-day life, and corruption and nepotism in society at large, which we witness in our own times.

Dr. William Albright, an archaeologist well-versed in the Hindu language, and James Grant calculated the Ages of the Hindu prophecies for themselves and concluded that the years between 1980 and 2000 would see great destruction.

In the second chapter of the *Shrimad Bhagwat*, Shree Sukdevji described the anti-cultural behavior, the corruption and nepotism of world that we see around us at the end of the Twentieth Century. Soon, he professes, the mind of all people will be filled with the virtuous thoughts and the desire to do good of the Supreme Intellect, whom Hindus personify as Kalki. When mankind so reforms, the Sat Yug will begin.

Harmony and equality among nations will be the opening wedge, say the *Valmiki Ramayan*, verses 95-106, and Shree Ramcharit Manas, meters 20-24. The growing unity in Europe as we head into the 1990's signals this time of change.

The Old Testament, set down centuries before the birth of Jesus, contains prophecies under the headings "Seven Times", and most of these have come true in the days since the time of Jesus. Both Daniel in the Old Testament and Revelation in the New, describe these times metaphorically. People will suffer from earthquakes, drought, epidemics, and more. Nature, itself, will seem out of balance. Nostradamus and other mystics collaborate the more ancient predictions.

To Moslems, the 20th Century of the Christian era coincides with the 14th Century of Islam, after which Kayamat, total destruction, will arrive.

Syed Kutub, in his Islamic commentary *The Hope of the Future*, states that the beginning of the 21st (Christian Era) Century will witness the union of physical science with religion. Mr. Kutub further quotes Dr. Kairel's book, *Unknown Man*, that a new cultural education system will replace all of the world's current educational systems. The new system of spiritual practices will cure many current mental diseases and end immorality.

In short, every one and every thing will be reborn. A new economic system will equalize all humanity. Social inequalities will vanish. The energies of science will turn from engines of destruction to the advancement of humankind.

Vinobaji Bhave, one of India's most famous politicians, who became a yogi and a social worker, wrote in *Koran SAR* that, in the days of the Kayamat, permanent sunlight, by which he meant intellectual enlightenment, will banish all darkness. The world will enjoy unprecedented peace.

In short, the world's four major religions concur that the enlightened future is at our door.

Chapter 3

Why is He Born In India?

India is a holy land, of Sages, Saints, ancient knowledge, and the holy River Ganges. The uniqueness of the Ganges has been confirmed by modern scientists: it preserves the freshness for good; it is insecticidal, destroying certain insects. More important, no other river in the world has inspired so many hermitages and religious institutions along its banks.

Many Saints live today in India. Each of India's twenty-two states can claim its own roster of living saints. In my own state, Gujarat, alone, saints like Shree Mahatma Jalaram, Shree Rang Avdhut, Shree Madhusudanji, Shree Shastriji, Shreemati Adrima, and Mahatmas of Manjusar have all achieved divine power and seen God. They lead those who hear them towards religion. When necessary, they have each performed miracles.

Mahatma Jalaram ran a Mission that provided food and other necessities to all--visitors, orphans, beggars, and the homeless. He never asked the cause of their misfortune.

God often tests His Saints, to prove their devotion, and mahatma Jalaram was a devotee of God. One day, God came to Mahatma Jalaram's shelter as a weak, old man who, himself, looked like a saint. Jalaram asked him to have lunch, but the "saint" refused.

"What would you like," Jalaram asked. "I am very weak and sick," the old man replied. "I can no longer look after myself. I need your wife to take care of me."

Mahatma Jalaram asked his wife if she would be willing to go with the old man to help him.

"It would give me great pleasure to be able to help him," she said. So she accompanied the old saint.

When they had travelled about a mile, he turned to her and said, "Please wait for me here. I will be back in a few minutes." He left his thick staff and knapsack with her and ambled off.

She waited a long time, but he did not return. Atfter a while she began to cry. Some children of a local shepherd heard her sobs. Cautiously, they ventured close.

"Why do you cry?" the oldest asked.

"Because a saint asked for my help," she replied, "and now he has gone on alone. Have I displeased him? Has some evil befallen him?" While the wife waited, still sobbing, the children ran to tell the story to Jalaram. As they finished, an oracle thundered from the sky, "Bravo, to Jalaram and his wife! For I, God, came as a weak, old saint to give you a test. Go and bring back your wife."

Those inside Jalaram's mission, friends and relatives cheered. They swarmed around him and, in a procession led by musical instruments, went to fetch his wife.

Throughout his long life, Jalaram performed countless miracles.

Three Arabs who served the Thakor [Ruler] of Rajakot, in the state of Gujarat, demanded a raise in pay.

"Since you guard my treasure," he replied, "I will offer you Rs.-18 each. If that does not please you, you may leave my employ."

"Twenty-two Rupees," they bargained.

"Eighteen," repeated the Thakor.

So the three men quit and started down the road to Junagadh. They killed some birds as they walked, stuffing them into their sacks.

As they passed through the town of Virpur, they met Mahatma Jalaram.

"Salam Alekum," they greeted him. "May peace be with you."

"Ram Ram," Jalaram properly replied. "Where are you heading?"

"To Junagadh," one Arab replied.

"That is far off," Jalaram said, "and it is evening already. I ask you to dine with me."

"But we are Muslims, and you are Hindu," another replied.

"That does not make any difference to me," Jalaram replied. "Ram [the Hindu name for God] and Rehman [the Muslim name for God] are one an the same. Come."

As they entered the mission, the Arabs grew fearful, for it violates Hindu law to eat meat or even to kill animals, and they carried the dead birds in their sacks.

"We must leave right after eating," they agreed, as they hung their sacks on a nail.

"No, no," Jalaram said when they rose to go. "You must stay the night."

"We cannot," they protested, afraid that the Hindu guests might learn their secret.

"Are you uneasy because of the sacks?" Jalaram asked, as he tapped them with a stick. "Do not be," he continued. "Simply open the sacks and allow the birds to fly free."

As one, the three Arabs looked to their sacks. They began to flutter. Together, they opened their sacks, and the birds flew to freedom.

The men fell to their knees.

"You are not Jalaram," they cried. "You are Allah! Forgive us!"

Now they gladly stayed the night. In the morning, one said to the other,

"He is Allah. We should ask Him whether we will get the jobs we seek in Junagadh."

"Good!" said another. "You ask".

"No, you!"

Trembling, one ventured, "Father Jalaram, we are hoping to get jobs with the Junagadh government. Will we get them?"

"You are not going to Junagadh," Jalaram said. "Messengers of the Thakor of Rajakot will be here any moment. He had refused you 22 Rs-., but now he will offer you 25 Rs.-"

Almost as he finished speaking, a messenger arrived, out of breath.

"The King wants you to return," he panted. "You have asked for 22 Rs.-, but, if you return now, with me, he offers you 25 Rs.-"

Another miracle! Again the Arabs bowed down and asked for Jalaram's blessing. They then left with the messenger, but all three returned to Jalaram's mission to ask for his blessing every year for as long as they lived.

It is said that God helped Narasih Mehta many times. He was very poor, for he spent all of his time worshipping God instead of working. Still, his daughter managed to marry into a fine family.

When it came time for her to host the ceremony to honor the birth of her first-born child, her in-laws asked what kinds of presents she would like her parents and guests to bring.

"Although," they said, "what kind of gifts could your father afford? He is as poor as a beggar . . . "

Still she wrote out the list that her in-laws dictated, until she had a list that only a king could afford.

"If your father can't afford what is on our list," her sister-in-law taunted, "let him bring two rocks."

Indeed God came as a relative of Narasih and did help, for she received every single thing on her list, plus two rocks--one of silver and one of gold, each weighing ten pounds.

Although Bharat (the original name for India) has many Saints who have performed countless miracles, let me focus in on Shree Shastriji. After years of devotion, Shree Shastriji received his first boon from the goddess Gayatri in March of 1975. His wish was that she should return every year on his birthday, and bless him. Every year she comes.

A few minutes before she arrives, the room fills with a divine fragrance.

Shree Shastriji grew up with the goddess' help.

He was born on September 7, 1932 at 12:00 p.m. In early October, his mother took sick and the doctor advised that the baby Shastriji should not drink from her milk. As he grew hungrier, his cries became more frantic. Desperately, an uncle took the child outside, for a walk.

As they passed the temple, he saw a lady sitting on the veranda.

"Give me the child," she said without ceremony. The uncle hesitated. He had never seen her before. She had spoken not a single word of introduction, yet, she held out her arms, and he passed the baby to her. She started feeding and continued to do so for the next ten days.

On the tenth day, the doctor pronounced the mother fit and ordered her to resume feeding. The uncle returned to the temple to thank the woman, but she was not there. She never gave a name, never left an address.

When Shree Shastriji was 24 years old, he began a search for this lady, all in vain.

Once, on his birthday, he asked the Shree Goddess Gayatri, "Who was that lady who fed me as a child? I have searched, but cannot find her anywhere."

You have found her, the goddess replied. It was I who succored you.

Shree Shastriji uses the powers granted him by the goddess to help the needy.

The moment Mataji Adrima's husband died, she began to recite the spell of the God of the Sun. For three days and nights she prayed continuously.

On the third day, the Sun God presented himself before her, as bright as a thousand suns. "I will offer you money", He said, "untold riches for the life of your husband."

"If pleases you," she answered, "I prefer the life of my husband."

So the Sun God granted her wish, and her husband blinked back to life.

"Before you go," she asked, "when shall I see God?"

"After the burglar", the Sun God replied.

Some time later, a thief broke into her house and stole her ornaments.

Not long after that, God presented Himself to her.

So much of Western culture traces its roots to India: arithmetic, art, astrology, silk, iron, many laws of science. Some of the great minds of the West--Max Muller, the American scholar Delbhare, Luie Jackroliyate, Victore Kosane--all who have studied the religions and culture of India, who have experienced them, reached the bottom of them--attest to the purity, greatness, and supremacy of them.

Of all the world's great religious books, wrote Mr. Luie Jakroliyat, in his book *Bible in India*, modern science totally corroborates only the account in the *Vedas*. The *Vedas'* orderly construction of the universe supports modern scientific theory.

The Prussian Minister to England, Baron Wilhem von Humbolt, considered the father of philosophy, in his book *On Gita* described the *Gita* as the best of all the world's Holy Books, one of which the whole world can be proud. Many who have read it would agree. Shree Ram Sharma has written an 18,000-page encyclopedia on the *Gita*.

Christopher Columbus left his home, his country, his continent to search for the richness, the grandeur, the prosperity of India. It was only by accident that he discovered America. Today, Native Red Americans he found still bear the name "Indians."

Western scholars wrote that, although the West regards India as a land of ancient religion, we fail to recognize the importance of the *Vedas*. Their presentation, they say, contains the perfect essence of religion. In addition, any modern student of the *Vedas* would know for certain that its authors knew about radio waves, electrons, even the airplane.

India once led the world in aerospace. Chapter 28 of the ancient book *Ansu Bodhini*, written millenia ago by Rushi Bhardhwaj, describes seven different kinds of aeirplanes in detail and discusses the science of aviation. Ancient Indian history describes gods, goddesses, sages, and kings travelling by different kinds of airplane.

It is written in the *Shrusut Sustrasthan*, Chapter 45/27, that Arya created the Sun Gem. He also created the Moon Gem, which has the power to heal sickness. The *Arin Akbari*, written in the Fifteenth Century, states that this kind of gem was used up to that time.

The civilization of ancient India may antedate any other by far. Most archeologists believe that the world's oldest traceable civilized tribes migrated from India.

J. MacMillan wrote, in *The Riddle of the Pacific*, that artifacts of the culture of India have been found on several Pacific islands.

Researchers uncovered a human idol in the desert of south Africa. In Indian fashion, it holds a bow in one hand and lighted torch in the other.

Robert Stone, president of the New England Activities Research Association, believed that an Indian tribe called Kalusa probably created the great pyramid of Misher.

A Shree Yantra [ceremonial platter that brings wealth] has been found in Russia. Scientists found a plate marked with secret, apparently occult, writing. Prof. Cuslov, of Moscow University, using a computerized, mathematics-based language analysis, detected a great similarity to the occult Shree Yantra of India. Therefore, Prof. Cuslov established, Indian arithmetic is well over 4,000 years old. He also believes that it was the ancient world's most advanced mathematical system, spread by early merchants all over the world.

You can find mistakes in statements generated by modern computers, but not one in the Vedic arithmetic system developed by Shree Sankaracharya of Puri. Furthermore, this arithmetical system proves to be very fast for performing large mental calculations. Dr. Andrew Nicholas, Senior Lecturer at London's Business School of Polytechnic, believes that we could devise a miraculous system of accounting based on Shree Sankaracharya's system.

Dutch, Portuguese, and English ships have plied the seas, carrying treasures from India, wrote the German poet Heinrich Heine in his *Book of Songs*, but we will bring the treasure of religious knowledge.

In short, many modern discoveries remind us that the civilization of ancient India permeated the ancient world. Will we come full cycle? Nostradamus, writing in France nearly 400 years ago, prophesied that the *Sat Yug*, the Age of Harmony, will come out of the Eastern country with water on three sides to lead us on to the next level of civilization.

India, alone among nations, can lay claim to the supreme wisdom that emanates from ancient books like the *Vedas* and the *Upandishads*. In them lie the secrets of yoga, which enable the truly dedicated to achieve whatever they want.

Not long ago, scientists believed that the atom was the smallest particle in nature. Now, scientists divide the atom into the electron, the proton, and the neutron. Thousands of years ago, Indian sages wrote that Nature has three fundamental elements: the tamogun, the force of Shiv (electron); the Rajogun, the force of Brahma (proton); and the Satogun, the force of Vishnu (neutron).

All ancient literature is written in the style of an epic, but it is true history. India launched the science of architecture. The Indian government recently discovered the evidence of the ancient palace of Lord Krishna, King of Dwarka City and the surrounding area, buried, like the legendary Atlantis, under fathoms of water off the coast of present-day Dwarka. To date they have uncovered the huge, magnificent fence that once surrounded the palace.

In the West Indian city of Ahmedabad, two Swinging Towers stand over five stories above the crowds who come to see them. If you should climb up one tower and give it a push, you will see the entire opposite tower swing in unison. Modern investigators can discover no force that links the towers.

Western architectural texts often recommend the minimum square footage for a specific room. Ancient Indian architecture recommends dimensions that bring harmony to those living in the house. The most responsive meditation room, for example, is 8' x 8'.

For the past five generations the Park Davis Co. has been a leader in medical science. Their research confirms that Indian surgeons have successfully practiced surgery for thousands of years. Their literature displays a reconstructed portrait of Shree Sushrut, an ancient Indian surgeon whose medical theories astounded the civilized world. In his book on anatomy, Shree Sushrut described the human body in detail--900 joints, 300 blood vessels, and 300 bones and another 300 veins, such as the famous *Ida, Pingla*, and *Suksma* veins which appear clearly with divine sight but which have yet to be discovered by modern science. He names medicines and describes their anesthetic and antiseptic properties.

Western military historians reviewing Indian literature surmised that Indian armies had a knowledge of weapons, including gases, which would astound a scientist of today. Some believe that Indian scientists may have invented the rocket and that today's rockets copy theirs.

Romare determined the speed of light in 1675; the U.S. physicist Albert Michelson calculated it as 186,864 miles per second in 1925. Yet, in the ancient Indian classic, the *Bhagwat*, Rushi Attreya lists the velocity of light as 187,670 m.p.s. Ancient Indian knowledge was, indeed, advanced and sophisticated.

Over two thousand years ago, Muni Kamvastyan wrote a textbook on sex, the *Kamshastra*, that at least rivals modern knowledge. Although modern doctors cannot describe how to determine the sex of a child at conception, Saint Kalidas' book *Muktshastra* does. On certain days at certain times of the day, intercourse creates a boy; at other specific times, a girl. He also explains how to predict the sex of any baby while in its mother's womb, a method that I and several of my friends have used successfully.

I have also witnessed the powerful effects of the ancient Aurvedic [Herbal] Medicine, an advanced science that has lay hidden for so long. Shree Iswarlal Vaidya cured three of my relatives from paralysis with a herbal medicine called "somal." His forefathers used somal before modern medicine knew that there might be a cure for paralysis.

In 1964 my wife, Lalita, had four attacks of high fever three months apart. Her doctor believed it was typhoid. Each time he administered the officially recommended medications she appeared to get better, but two months later the fever returned. The fourth time her temperature soared to 104.5. The doctor administered a medicine to bring it down quickly. Perspiration poured from her body. We had to change her soaking wet clothes twice within what seemed like a few minutes. Then her temperature dropped so low that the thermometer registered nothing. Her body felt cold. In near panic I called for the doctors.

Five doctors responded. The conventional physicians administered a large dose of conventional medicine through a hypodermic needle. We waited. Nothing happened.

Then herbal-Aurvedic Doctor Shree Navalbhai put a dot of herbal medicine the size of a period (".") on her tongue and within minutes her temperature began to rise. He continued to treat her with an herbalistic medicine made with thin, gold foil, and her fever has never returned.

Modern pharmacologists could increase their knowledge dramatically with the plants that grow wild in the Himalayas. The magazine *Akhand Anand* reports that a hiker who cleaned his teeth with the branch of one specific tree that grows there found that minutes later all of his teeth came out, with no pain and no bleeding. Properly harnessed, the medicines in this branch could save untold dollars and misery among those who need dental extractions.

On the other hand, a well-known photographer from the State of Gujarat, India, went to the Himalayas to photograph a valley of flowers. So taken with the beauty of one flower in particular, he bent to sniff its fragrance and died within seconds.

A gentlemen in Rajkot in the State of Gujarat, extracts bad teeth with no medicine whatsoever. I watched him work once. He moved his patient's head three or four times, stopping in certain definite positions. Then he easily removed the teeth with neither pain nor blood.

"You could become a millionaire," I said to him.

He smiled.

"This is a gift from God," he answered, "not a business."

The student of yoga spends years awakening his or her Serpent (Kundalini) power. Yet, the touch of a Saint awakened mine within a few minutes.

I tried to do the same for my wife.

"How does it feel?" I asked.

"Like an electric current passing through my body," she replied. "And I saw a Divine Light through closed eyes."

I stopped at once, recognizing this method's danger, and have never tried it again on anyone because I did not know how to control the Serpent power. Although I could raise the power up, if the power of the Serpent rises too fast, the patient can die or go mad. Only a Saint or one with Divine Power can bring this power "back down."

In the late 1980's scientists learned that a child can be trained while still in the womb. However, King Prahlad was taught in the womb by his mother, Kayahud. Luv and Kush, sons of Lord Shree Ram, were taught in the womb by his Mother Sita five thousand years ago. Four hundred years ago, King Sivaiji was trained by his mother, Tarabai. There are so many similar examples in Indian history.

Without effective organizations behind them, most religions would remain isolated cases of inspiration. Similarly, in society only law and social decorum keep us from degenerating into anarchy. However, to the extent that individuals reject law and decorum, disorder still reigns.

On the other hand, the Vedic, or Hindu, religion conveys the message of internal peace; from this message flows its eternal strength. This fountain of eternal strength benefits all humanity.

The student of Indian literature senses the strength that flows to and from those who tap this ancient source of knowledge. In our secular age the magic of India has lost some of its appeal; however, the well-spring of that knowledge has not failed. If too many of our individual lives pass unhappily, perhaps our craving for the physical at the expense of the spiritual has poisoned our social structure.

In his book, *Ideas on the Philosophy of the History of Mankind*, the German scholar Johann Gotfield comments on the ideal character of Indian civilization. Mankind should have originated in India, he says, where simplicity and humility are considred the first steps toward knowledge.

The ancient Sanskrit language is so rich that Indians call it the language of the Gods. Scholars call grammar the first and most important science, because communication is the foundation of all other sciences. Sanskrit has rendered eminent service to Western philology, for it first analyzed word forms and recognized the difference between linguistic prefixes, roots, and suffixes in a system of grammar more accurate and complete than that of any other language. NASA has recognized it as the one natural language that can render ideas with the precision of current artificial language.

The Western word "Amen" may have its roots in the Indian "Oam". Similarly, the ancient Greek word "Christ", meaning "messiah", may have come from the Sanskrit word "Krishna".

Ancient Indian knowledge grew from a fusion of meditation and science. Shree Ram Sharma grew up amidst this ancient source of knowledge and culture.

"Oh Bharat [India]," promised Lord Krishna in the *Gita*, "whenever virtue declines and evil predominates, I will appear Incarnate in visible form to destroy evil and re-establish virtue" (IV: 7-8).

The science of astronomy originated in India. It is one of the six important subordinate branches of the Vedas. The Vedas indicate that Hindus knew that the earth rotated on its axis and of the procession of the equinoxes into distant eras. Some Westerners believe that India inherited astrology from the Greeks who in turn borrowed it from the civilization of central Asia. The observatories were built in old ancient days in Delhi Jaipur, Mathura, Ujjai and Varanasi. The famous sun temple of Konark was used for this very purpose. Seven stories and twenty-seven windows of Qutub Minar in Delhi were meant for the observation of seven planets and twenty-seven constellation respectively.

Acupressure therapy was known in India over 3000 years ago. Mr. Devendra Vora, author of *Health In Your Hand* went deep into it and found its roots in India as far back as 3000 years ago.

Yoga means not only exercise and meditation, yoga is the union of the individual soul with God through scientific methods. Sages of ancient India went so deep into the human body that they found life-giving electricity (chetna, Prana, etc.) and other centers in one human body. By developing them one can be a superman.

God has sent a Messiah in the person of Shree Ram Sharma Acharya to earth to finish the work of the ancient sages and to bring harmony, and the light of ancient Indian culture, religion, and knowledge of Hindu civilization to the world, it was God's wish that he is born in India.

Chapter 4

Childhood

In Agra, near Dehli, stands the famous Taj Mahal, one of the seven wonders of the world. Its name is written in gold in the history of India.

About 23 kilometers north of Agra, in a small village named Amvalkheda, a child was born to a Brahmin on September 21, 1911. His parents named the baby Shree Ram.

His father was Rupsharma, one of the greatest scholars of his time in the *Bhagwat*. The *Bhagwat* is one of India's two greatest epics--explaining the soul, and the political and cultural value of life. Shree Rupsharma's family was well to do, and young Shree Ram Sharma often accompanied his father as he traveled to the rulers of many princely states to deliver religious discourses on the *Bhagwat*.

Shree Ram Sharma's primary education began in the village school. He learned Sanskrit, however, from his father. Sanskrit is the most ancient language of India, the one in which all ancient Indian books were written. By the time he was eight, Shree Ram could quote the poetic meter of the Ramayan from memory.

At the age of eight, Shree Ram experienced "Yagnopavit," performed by Shree Madan Mohan

Malaviyaji. Yagnopavit, the sacred thread ceremony, is a child's first step into the Hindu religion. At the ceremony, Shree Madan Mohan Malaviyaji asked the young Shree Ram to recite the five Mala of Goddess Gayatri's spell, or "Mantra".

In Sanskrit, "Gayatri" is the name given by Saints, thousands of years ago, to the Creator and Universal God. "Mala" are "rosaries" composed of 108 beads made from different kinds of woods or precious stones.

From early childhood, Shree Ram felt drawn to the Himalayan Mountains. One day, in his ninth year, he left home, telling no one, and marched to the railway station.

"What brings you here?" the station master asked.

"I am going to the Himalaya!" the open-hearted child replied.

Elders of his village tell that Shree Ram led an unusual childhood. Many times, instead of returning home, as he should have, from school, he would stop to help someone or to meditate under a tree. Even as a child, he felt the urge to help the poor and needy fight against social problems.

When he was 13 years old, the elders tell, an old Harijan-a member of the "untouchable" caste--lady of his village took sick with severe diarrhea. She had neither family nor friends to help her, so Shree Ram vowed that he would.

He got medicine for her from the village doctor. He brought her food, secretly, from his own house. He washed her dirty and spoiled clothes. He worked in secret, for in that society any who would help--or even touch--a Harijan would, himself, be cast out. Indeed, when his family and the people of the village found out, they did cast him out. They forced him from the house, made him sleep out of doors, and refused to touch him. Yet he did not stop helping her.

Within 15 days, the old lady was cured. She declared that God had sent Shree Ram to help her and blessed him from the depth of her heart. As time passed, his family, friends, and society gradually accepted him back.

One one occasion, his mother wanted five Brahmins to join them for lunch. As she prepared the meal, she asked Shree Ram to go and bring five Brahmins. Instead, Shree Ram returned with five very poor people, suffering from leprosy and leucoderma. His mother was disappointed.

"But Mother," Shree Ram argued, "these five needed the charity more."

She had to agree, and finally served them. Shree Ram believes that what one gives should be given to the truly needy.

Shree Ram always took time to help his neighbors. Before leaving for the market, he would check with his neighbors to see what they might need. When asked why, he would answer politely, "Since I am going for my own needs, what difference does it make to me if I also get something for them?"

While growing up, he met Mahatma Gandhi, the father of the Indian nation. Gandhi believed in the power of truth expressed through non-violence. His beliefs guided India to independence from British rule. Gandhi's followers named him "Mahatma," meaning "Great Soul."

Many believed that Mahatma Gandhi could perform miracles, Shree Ram among them. He joined Gandhi's "Ashram" to learn how to perform miracles. In an "Ashram", one leads a disciplined, monastic life. Shree Ram performed his duty efficiently and enthusiastically.

One day Gandhi asked Shree Ram, "Didn't you come here with the intention to learn how to become Gandhi?"

"Yes," Shree Ram confessed.

"Did you learn anything," Gandhi asked, "or not?"

Shree Ram described his program during the last three months of his stay at the Ashram.

Gandhi smiled. "What you have accomplished here in three months," Gandhi replied, "is, itself, enough to become Gandhi."

Mahatma Gandhi recognized the light of eagerness in Shree Ram's eyes. He told Shree Ram a tale of a scientist named Thomas Humphrey Davy.

Although born into a poor family, Davy yearned to become a scientist. Too poor to attend school, he begged his mother, "Mummy will you please take me to any scientist's house where I will do his housework and also try to learn whatever he would teach me." However, try as she might, she met only rejection.

Finally, one scientist agreed to hire the boy to clean house. Davy worked hard, filled with enthusiasm. He asked questions that often led to long, full explanations, and to discussions about test results. The scientist found young Davy a hard worker, with good concentration, a logical approach to problems, and an eagerness to learn. Thomas Humphrey Davy began to help the scientist with his research, along with the housework, and went on to surpass his master as a great scientist. His inventions include the "safety lamp" that enabled miners to light their way without exploding dangerous gases.

"The responsibilities that you were given here," Gandhi concluded to Shree Ram, "were to increase your sense of responsibility and your enthusiasm. Even I have this same task here. If you take this approach to every task in your life, you will succeed gloriously, whether your path be political, religious, or social. This is the only way to succeed."

The thought of doing miracle vanished from Shree Ram's mind. He determined, instead, to develop the positive virtues that were the true inner source of Gandhi's powers.

After returning home, he tackled any task that he assumed with eager dedication. He kept the ideals of great men ever before him. Yet he credited his successes to the grace of God.

HIS MASTER AND HIS VISION

The Himalayas are the home of many powerful and great Munis, Rushis, and Saints. These men have achieved such great inner strength (sidhi) they can accomplish anything that lies within the rules of God.

When Shree Ram was fifteen, while deep in prayer, he saw one of these Great Saints robed in Divine Light. Was it a ghost? He rubbed his eyes to see if he might be dreaming. The vision remained, hanging like a picture on a wall.

This body bathed in Divine Light began to speak to him. "I have guided your soul for your last three lives," it began. "Now that you have passed from childhood, I have come to give you guidance.

"So far, you have no memory of your previous lives; that is why you are frightened. I shall help you to relive your previous incarnations and to dispel all your doubts."

The Saint put Shree Ram in a deep meditation and began to show him his past three lives, as if he were living them rather than dreaming or recalling. The three lives passed as movies before his eyes.

Shree Ram saw himself born as Saint Kabir, in the year 1398, to an unwed, Brahmin girl in a Hindu family. With no husband to provide for them, she abandoned the child on the bank of a pond. There, a Moslem weaver found him and raised the child as his own son. He named the boy Kabir.

Kabir believed strongly in God and devoted himself to God's ways. Kabir tried hard to reform society. He opposed, and succeeded in changing some of the evil customs of that Hindu society. His angry opponents tried to kill him. They bound his hands and feet with iron chain and threw him into a river. Miraculously, the chains snapped and Kabir survived. He continued his battle against erroneous beliefs in the tradition of the great Rushis and Saints.

Soon many devotees, both Hindus and Moslems, became his disciples.

When Saint Kabir died in 1518, his Hindu followers wanted to cremate his body according to their custom; his Moslem followers wanted to bury him according to theirs. Arguments broke out among the factions. Then a second miracle occurred: the dead body of Kabir, as it lay beneath its white burial cloth, disappeared and turned into flowers. His Hindu followers cremated some of the flowers and his Moslem followers buried the rest.

Saint Ramdas became his second birth. During this life, from 1608 to 1682, he helped the powerful Maratha King Chhatrapti Shivaji consolidate the fragmented southwestern section of India into a single kingdom. King Chhatrapti Shivaji introduced schools for physical education into even his smallest villages. His people prospered happily, because religion and respect for life became the rule.

Then famine struck the land. Proudly, Shivaji showed Ramdas how he helped the suffering by dispensing food and providing jobs. Without me, he bragged to the Ramdas, so many would have died of starvation.

Take this hammer, Saint Ramdas told Shivaji, and strike this large rock that stands next to you.

Shivaji struck the rock. The rock cracked, and out jumped a live frog.

How can that be, the startled Shivaji asked, that a frog could live in so hard a rock.

It is because, Saint Ramdas answered calmly, someone more powerful than you helped the frog.

King Shivaji's ego vanished.

His third incarnation, as Shree Ramkrishna Paramhans, occurred from 1836 to 1887. Shree Ramkrishna lived, with his wife, in Calcutta. He lived the life of a saint and helped to re-awaken Indian culture and tradition.

Among those awakened by Shree Ramkrishna's call was Swami Vivekanand, who travelled throughout India to spread the religious awakening.

In America, at a world religious conference, Swami Vivekanand lectured on Indian religion, custom and tradition, greatly impressing the minds of all members of the conference.

Shree Ram reflected on the visions on his past three lives. He hoped that he had not been deceived. Rather than question, however, Shree Ram chose to observe and watch for an answer. The Divine figure in the vision, the Swami Sarveshwaranandji, whom we shall refer to as Dada Gurudev, read his thoughts and spoke from the vision:

"God will test His servants before He makes Himself known unto them. He has been watching for one who can advance the welfare of all people, for this era suffers from distress, and still there is risk of greater calamity befalling humanity.

"You will be His medium. Heretofore, you have thought yourself a common man living a common life. For this reason I have shown you your past three lives and how you have used them to benefit mankind.

"This is your fourth birth. As before, I will help you in your labors. Today many banter the name of God, call themselves Saints, and hypnotize their followers for personal gain. We must combat this.

"It is good that you are married, for in this age the bachelor has few benefits and more risks. Your 'birth helper' from your last two incarnations has joined you, again as your wife. She will look after the administration of the institute you shall find. In your last two incarnations you have only your wife to rely on; but in keeping with todays needs, you will have all faculties and support from thousands of people to bring in a revolutionary new era."

Dada Gurudev explained in detail what Shree Ram must do:

"First, you must do 24 Gayatri Maha-purushcharan in 24 years [Note: 7,000 recitations of the Gayatri Mantra per day, following the prescribed rules and manners, every day for 365 days constitute one Mahapurushcharan].

"During these 24 Mahapurushcharan, you may eat only of bread made from barley and buttermilk twice a day.

"Third, you must continuously burn a lamp fueled with Ghee [made by melting butter at a prescribed heat].

"Periodically, from now on, you must come to the Himalayas, in a place close to me, for further guidance. These periods may last six months to a year.

"And finally, you must become a freedom fighter for the independence of India."

As he listened and observed, Shree Ram acquired a feeling of oneness, as though he and Dada Gurudev had two separate bodies but shared just one soul. His doubts had melted. Shree Ram vowed to have no desires of his own, but to support the goals of Dada Gurudev, even should they cost him his own life.

For sixty years, he has maintained that direction, never questioning whether what was asked is possible, never questioning whether he could accomplish it, never faltering.

Now he had seen the complete picture of his life cycle. The vision pleased Shree Ram. He gave himself, with his purest heart and soul, saying "I am offering to you whatever I have. I have never seen God, but you work for the welfare for all people as God would do, and so you are as my God. The path to the success of these goals I shall not neglect."

Dada Gurudev issued two clear instructions.

"First, no matter what others say or do, you must move ahead toward new achievement with all your determination. Second, start performing penance to make yourself more pure and humble. Thereby shall you develop an inward power that shall guide you spiritually. Furthermore, you must use this Divine Power for the welfare of all peoples and never simply for yourself."

Shree Ram needed no further elaboration. He did not ask about births before those he was shown nor of those in between. Enough that Dada Gurudev, himself, would hold his hand, sit in the same boat, and keep his faith from tottering.

In order to overcome the limitations of the physical body, to inspire and encourage others, it is necessary to transcend the physical body and to enter an astral body.

"Your Physical body will work until more is needed," Dada Gurudev continued. "Thereafter you will leave this physical body and enter into your astral body. At appropriate times, I shall introduce you to the great saints living in the Himalayas at a spiritual, immovable place where spiritual vibrations reach a crescendo. Both of us will bide there together and help you to make astral bodies like a physical body. You will also come to know the saints who live there, how they live, and how you are going to live there. In short, this is why you shall be called four times to the Himalayas: for the lessons you must learn and the tests that you must pass."

"In ancient days, Saints and Rushis lived mostly between the mouth of the River Ganges and Rushikesh. Now, so many temples that attract so many devotees and tourists have sprung up there, that the Holy Ones have moved higher up on the mountain."

"An accomplished mystic named Madame Blavatski," said Shree Ram, "believed that she could keep in touch with her astral body. She wrote in one of her books that in these Himalayas lives a Parliament of great saints that she called the 'Invisible [Government] Helpers'."

"Yes," Dada Gurudev answered, "It is true, and you will be able to see with your own, naked eyes, all of these saints when you visit my dwelling in the mountains. However, wait for my call. Do not come just for curiosity. You will be called when you are needed and when you are ready for the Test. Once you have pledged your self to me, your life is my responsibility."

With that, Dada Gurudev disappeared.

Shree Ram began to follow the regimen laid out by his Gurudev. He changed his eating and drinking and began to recite the Gayatri Mantra. His family objected.

"Please," they begged, "Don't cause any trouble. Just eat your food and live your life the way normal people do.

"You are lucky," they told him, "you have inherited a great fortune. Generations could live on what you have inherited without lifting a finger. Still, you should work and earn money. Save your ancestral fortune for future needs."

Shree Ram grew tired of their harping. He kept silent and went about his tasks quietly, in a way that left him answerable only to himself. This helped him to reach his goal.

Chapter 5

First Call of Gurudev

Written by Shree Ram Sharma Acharya and translated by Shree Satyanarayan Pandya.

Not even a year had passed when I received an invitation from within me to visit the Himalayas. Although I was not in a hurry, I was anxious, no doubt to see that which was, till then, unseen. Others would not have even considered visiting that region in that season, facing hardship, loneliness and wild animals. I had to wage a great war against the evil thoughts of fear and the desire to continue my safe and secure life without these hazardous risks. This state of dilemma lasted hardly twenty-four hours. I informed my family members and started my journey the next day. They kept mum, for they knew that I did not alter my decisions. It has been my practice to appear in tough examination and get a good reward.

My first visit to the Himalayas was my first association with it. I had no prior information about the conditions I would be required to face there. In those days, bus service ran from Devprayag to Uttar-kashi only. The entire distance from Rushikesh to Devprayag, and the rest of the journey from Uttarkashi, had to be crossed on foot. I had no idea how much baggage I could carry on my back. I had taken some more luggage which I had to distribute to fellow travellers, while retaining only that which was essential and which I could carry.

Gurudev wanted to test my capacity to face adverse circumstances so my journey became increasingly difficult. Anyone else placed in those circumstances would have become nervous, turned back, or fallen ill. However Gurudev wanted to teach me the practical lesson that adversity can be faced and even turned to advantage if the mind is strong. To achieve significant success in life, man has to be strong.

It is said that in the old days Rushis lived in the region between Rushikesh and Gomukh and that the region above Gomukh was the abode of Gods. Conditions, however, changed after the Ice Age, and Gods entered their astral bodies and now roam through space. Rushis of ancient ages have shifted to the region above Gomukh. The region below Gomukh is now visited by tourists. Although there are some cottages here and there, it is difficult to find anyone who may be called a Rushi.

I had heard that Yogis with supernatural powers lived in caves in the Himalaya region, but I did not find it to be true. It is a difficult region in which to make a living. People visit casually, but they do not stay here. I learned from some Sadhus, young pretenders to the study of yoga who make a show of pretending to be devotees, that they were there for curiosity and what they could beg from tourists. They had no philosophical background, and their style of living was hardly that of ascetics. Shortly after making contact, they would express their physical needs. I felt unhappy and marched ahead thinking how could such people provide spiritual satisfaction to pilgrims who passed.

In comparison, I found the owners of small shops in the resting places to be much better. They were simple, good people. If one purchased flour, other grains, or rice, they provided cooking utensils free of cost. They sold tea, matches, gram flour, jaggery, or potatoes to the travellers. Pilgrims were often devoted, but poor. Locally made blankets could be rented for the night.

Enduring the winter cold and walking so far were difficult tests. In this season residents, Sadhus, and hermits shift to the lower regions to make their livings and graze their cattle. Utter silence reigned in cottages of the villages. I faced these difficulties as I journeyed from Uttar-kashi to Nandanvan.

It was lonely, with no facilities for boarding or lodging. Wild animals roamed freely. The wind blew cold. The sun remained hidden behind the hilltops until about 10 a.m. It disappeared behind the mountain peaks about 2 p.m. Although the sun shone on the peaks, there was dim darkness on the paths below. Hardly anyone crossed my path. People moved about only on urgent tasks, such as the death of a relative. From every point of view, I was alone in that region. My only companions were a palpitating heart and an alert mind. I was being put to the test, to see whether I could undertake so long a journey under such circumstances. My heart resolved that I could not die so long as there was no one to kill me. My mind told me that there was life in trees and other

*vegetation. Birds live on vegetation. Fish live in water.
Wild animals wander in the forest. They remain alone
and quite naked. I told myself, "When so many
creatures live in this region, how could it be called
deserted or lonely? Do not belittle yourself, for you
believe that the whole world is one family. How can you
feel lonely in the presence of so many creatures? Why
regard man alone as a living being? Are these
creatures not part and parcel of your own self?"*

*My pilgrimage continued and, with it, my
thinking. As man is in the habit of living in a
community, he fears loneliness. Darkness is another
big cause of fear. Throughout the day, man lives in
light. In the night he lights lamps to dispel darkness.
But darkness combined with loneliness is that much
more frightening. A yogi must conquer these fears.
The ability to conquer fear has been regarded as an
important step on the path to spirituality.*

*Another danger in this noiseless Himalayan
region was the wild animals who move about freely in
the still of the night in search of food. An encounter
with such nocturnal animals amounted to a direct
confrontation with death. When there was no noise
and utter desolation, such animals came out even by
day in search of prey and water. I had to face all these
difficulties on this journey.*

*During my nights, I met crawling black snakes
and hissing pythons. Small lions are found in this
area, more swift, if less powerful, than those found on
the plains. Among those animals who live mainly on
vegetation, the bear is the most aggressive. Wild
elephants are found in the Shivalik range and lower
ranges of the Himalayas. All of them by nature keep to*

themselves unless one meets them face-to-face or unless they are teased or otherwise provoked. They will charge if they have the slightest feeling of fear or anger.

Pilgrims must often face pythons, snakes, iguanas, bears, panthers, tigers, and elephants. Animals leave the track and keep their distance when they find people in a group, but they hold their course when they see a man alone. In that event the man would be wise to seek another route.

Such confrontations might occur ten to twenty times each day. Seeing me alone, they moved fearlessly. They did not leave the path; I had to in order to save myself. This sound simple in the retelling, but it was extremely difficult in practice, for each encounter appeared to be an actual encounter with death. Sometimes these animals walked with me and sometimes they followed me. Fear of death is most terrifying. Although they may not charge, the very sight of them appeared to be as dreadful as death, itself. When one has to face such an encounter almost every hour, palpitations of the heart were bound to increase. These ferocious animals often moved in a herd. If they had attacked, they would have cut me into pieces, clawed my flesh, ended my existence.

Once again, I had to summon courage and foresight. Death is, no doubt great, but not greater than life. If there is a feeling of fearlessness and cordiality within, the violence of even ferocious animals is cooled, and even their nature is changed. During this whole journey, there were about three to four hundred such confrontations, but I summoned my courage every time and assumed a demeanor of carefree *friendliness. I thought that the time of death is predetermined. Why should I not face death happily if I have to die here, in such circumstance? Why should I be afraid of it? I had to force these thoughts on myself. Loneliness, darkness, and messengers of death combined to frighten me and warn me to turn back, but my determination came to my rescue every time, and my pilgrimage kept advancing.*

Was I being put to the test to see if I could conquer loneliness? In a few days, my heart became strong and the creatures of that region became my own kith and kin. Fear disappeared, loneliness became likable, and thus commenced the first of a series of successes, like answering the first question right on an exam paper.

The next question was that of winter. I thought, when the mouth, nose, eyes, head, ears and hands, which usually remain uncovered, did not catch cold, why should the rest of me feel cold? In Norway, Finland and regions of the North Pole the temperature is always below zero, and yet Eskimos and people of other communities live there. Here in the Himalayas the altitude was only ten to twelve thousand feet. I thought that things are not so difficult here and ways can be found to seek protection from cold. I came to learn from a local man that it is very cold on the outer surface of the mountains, but inside the many caves was comparative warmth. Certain specific types of shrubs burn easily although they are green. Certain vegetables can be eaten raw. The knots that grow on the steam of a birch tree, when boiled, make a tea which warms the body. If one sits on his feet so that his head touches his knees, he will not feel much cold. Feeling more or less cold depends a lot on one's imagination. Children run here and there scantily clothed. Yet they feel no discomfort. It may not hold true for old, sick people, but a young man is not apt to die of cold. By adopting these measures and controlling one's thoughts, the chill become tolerable. Entertaining a lot of positive thoughts also helped.

One more thing about violent animals. Their eyes shine when they move about, mostly at night. All animals, even lions, are afraid of human beings. If a person is not afraid of them and they are not teased, they do not attack human beings. They can thus be turned into friends.

In the beginning, I was afraid of them. Then I recalled how wild animals are tamed and trained to perform miraculous feats in a circus. I had read the description of a European lady from Tanzania whose husband worked for the Forest Department. She had tamed two small tiger cubs that had separated from their parents. They used to sleep in her lap even after they had fully grown up. If one controls fear and feels love, a person can enjoy living in a dense forest.

Natives often live in dense forests and fear nothing in it. Remembering this, I conquered my fear and thought that a day would come when I would live in a cottage in the forest and that the cow and tiger would drink from the same watering place.

The mind can be weak. It can also be powerful, if properly trained. I drove fear from my mind and continued my pilgrimage through the region. Instead of expecting favorable circumstances, I concentrated on making my mind strong. I molded my mind in this direction, and adverse circumstances which, in the beginning appeared dreadful, became easy and natural.

My mind came under my full control by constant beating, thrashing, and molding during this pilgrimage of twenty days. I started feeling as if I had lived in this region all my life.

Up to Gangotri, pedestrians had worn a precarious path. However, Tapovan lies in a flat plain, well up into the mountains, with not even a foot-path through the vegetation. One must walk according to inner inspiration or rely on fate. After Tapovan, there is a series of high mountains, and then one can reach Nandanvan. This is the place to which I was summoned.

I reached there at the proper time and saw Gurudev standing before me. My joy knew no bounds. The first time we met, he had visited my house. This time I came to his abode. How I wish that this chain of meetings might continue throughout my life.

This time I had been put to three tests: to live alone, to endure the wild fury of winter weather, and to live with wild animals without fear. I succeeded in all three tests.

Gurudev said it was necessary to have strong will and to develop spiritual power. Adverse circumstances should be transformed into favorable ones. A person with the soul of a Rushi should not fear death, so what is there to fear about lions and tigers? You have spent most of your time under dangerous conditions.

Out talks did not last long.

I was taken to the cave in which he made his abode and was shown a place to sleep. I slept very soundly, perhaps two or three times longer than I normally slept. The fatigue and weariness of the journey disappeared as if I had not walked any distance at all.

I took a bath there in a flowing stream and then performed a worship ceremony called *sandhya*. Therein, I saw the Supreme Divine Lotus and Supreme Root for the first time in my life. The fragrance of the brahma-kamal [Supreme Divine Lotus, which grows only in a special place in the Himalayas] draws one immediately into a brief meditative state. The Supreme Root is dug from the earth. It looks like a yam and tastes like a water-nut. It weights about five pounds and satisfies hunger for about a week. These two were the only tangible presents from Gurudev. One helped in eradicating physical fatigue and the other in infusing the mind with spirituality.

Then I cast a glance at Tapovan. The entire plateau appeared to be covered with a velvet-like carpet of flowers. There had been, as yet, no heavy snow fall. Heavy snows make the flowers ripen, wither, and spread their seeds, ready to sprout the next season.

Interview with the Rushis
in the Inaccessible Himalayas

The first day passed viewing the supreme power in the natural beauty of Nandanvan. I did not realize when the sun set and night approached. I was directed to go to a specific nearby cave and prepare for sleep. The idea was to send me to a safer place so that my body might not be exposed to the fury of bitter cold. There was a possibility of meeting Gurudev again in the night.

Gurudev suddenly appeared that night in the cave. The bright, golden light of the full moon scattered its light across the Himalayas. The arrival of Gurudev formed a circle of warmth; otherwise, it would have been difficult to come out in that terribly stormy night.

I did not ask the purpose of his visit. I knew that Gurudev was showering his kindness on me for some specific purpose. I followed him.

My feet moved above the surface. I realized that day why it was necessary to acquire the supernatural power of soaring through the air, of walking in space. It was more difficult to walk on those rough and rugged glacial surfaces than to walk on top of water. Today, the traveller in the Himalayas may not need such supernatural transportation, but it was definitely needed in those days to cross those horrible, hostile regions.

I stepped out of the cave into the bitter cold and started moving in mid air over the golden Himalayas as if I were his tail. The purpose of today's pilgrimage was to introduce me to the tapasthali, where the ancient Rushis performed penance. All had abandoned their physical bodies, but most of them had retained their astral bodies. I suddenly found myself kneeling, with folded hands, and my head bowed in a position of deferential salutation. I was being introduced to the Rushis living today in their astral bodies in the Himalayas. This night was extremely important to me and I have felt fortunate all my life.

Earlier, during my journey through the Himalayas, I had seen only those caves which were easily approachable. I realized at this moment that there was far more unseen than I had witnessed so

*far. Small caves belonged to wild animals, but larger
ones were clean, neat and orderly and were meant for
the Rushis living in their astral bodies. Their past
association sometimes draws them there.*

*All the Rushis were in a meditative pose.
Gurudev told me that they often lived in such a state,
not breaking their meditation for any reason. Their
astral bodies were presented to me along with their
names. This was the wealth, the unique magnificence
of this region.*

*They all knew beforehand of my visit with
Gurudev. So as we appeared before them, each opened
his eyes and, with a gentle smile on his face, nodded
slightly in response to our adorations. There was no
conversation with any of them. If a person living in an
astral body has anything to convey, he does it by inner
speech, that is, by inspiration. The purpose of this
day's meeting was only to see them, not to say
anything or to listen to them. A new student who had
come to join the class was to be introduced, so that he
could be helped along, if need be. Probably the Rushis
had already been informed what I, a relative child,
could do in the future in my own way to help fulfil their
incomplete work.*

*An astral body can arouse inner inspiration and
transmit power currents. Only a person still in a
physical body, however, can give direct, verbal advice.
Divine powers, therefore, select some physical person
to convey messages. Until that night, I had been the
medium of expression for only one guide, but now all of
these divine souls could utilize me to provide
inspiration to other people. For this reason, Gurudev
was introducing me to each of them, and each, in*

turn, without wasting a precious moment or observing formalities, was indicating his acceptance of this request. In this manner, my divine pilgrimage continued through the night. Before dawn, Gurudev left me back in my cave and returned to his dwelling.

I saw the place of the ancient Rushis for the first time that night. I had passed holy places, ponds and rivers earlier in this journey, but not until then did I know which Rushi was associated with a particular place. This I saw now for the first and last time.

Before sending me back, Gurudev told me, "Do not try to establish contact with these Rushis of your own accord, lest you interfere with their work. If they have any directions to give, they will make contact themselves. Your contact with me has always been the same: you will not, on your own initiative, knock on my door. Whenever necessary, I shall approach you myself, make known my purpose, and arrange all necessary resources.

"Do not regard the wonders which you have seen here as mere curiosities. All of these great, divine souls will fulfill their goals through you--whatever they cannot perform themselves for lack of physical bodies. It has been the tradition to establish mass contacts through the medium of some competent person like you. Henceforth you will regard instructions of these Rushis as if they came from me, and perform whatever you are directed to do."

What could I say, except to signal my acceptance? Gurudev disappeared.

Clarification of Outline of Future Program

The next day the journey through Nandanvan became even more wonderful. The recollection of seeing so many Rushis and Gurudev during the previous night moved before my eyes like a film. As the sun spread across the velvety carpet of Nandanvan, it appeared as if heaven had descended upon Earth. So many flowers of many colors were thickly packed and scattered throughout the plateau. It appeared as if a green carpet with unique mosaic had been spread before me.

All of a sudden Gurudev appeared. Unlike last night, he was in the same form of mass light in which he had first appeared before me in my room of worship.

"I was aware of your devotion and your courage in past lives," Gurudev said. "This time I called you here, put you to three tests, and examine you to determine whether you are fit to undertake more important tasks. I have remained with you throughout this journey and have been watching all that happened and your reactions and I am fully convinced. If your mental background had not been strong and reliable, the Rushis who live in this region in their astral bodies would have not appeared before you and expressed their concern for the state of the world. They want the work yet undone to be completed. Great persons do not disclose their minds before weak or incompetent people. They have disclosed their concerns to you, deeming you competent.

"If your surrender to their goal is real, you must carry out their agenda with all your heart. The first

Program is to perform 24 purushcharans of the Gayatri Mantra in 24 years. Great tasks demand great competence, and so you have been entrusted with this first program. The second Program is two-fold: You must continue your studies and then take your pen in your hand to translate the books of the ancient sages and then arrange for their publication, to make them easily available to the masses. This will revive a divine culture which has almost become extinct and to erect the structure of the future civilization of the world. At the same time, so long as your physical body lives, you must write books which may be made easily available to all in as many languages as possible and thereby help bring heaven to Earth. This work is linked to the power that you have just acquired. In due course, thoughtful and competent people will join you who will help you finish the work that you, in turn, must leave incomplete.

"The third Program is to play both a direct and indirect role as a freedom fighter in the fight for India's independence. This struggle will last until 1947. By that time, most of your acts of penance from your First Phase will be completed. People will hear of its achievements. At present, there is no indication that the British will easily grant independence to India and go home. However independence is bound to come to pass even before the purushcharans are completed. By that time, you will have gained the full scope of knowledge you will need to change the present era and rebuild society.

"A purushcharans should culminate in a Yagna ceremony. A Mahayagna in lieu of 24 purushcharans should be so large that 2.4 million sacrificial offerings

should be given to the sacred fire, so that, through its purifying medium, you may lay the foundation of an organization. This will require an investment of millions of rupees and the cooperation of millions of people. Do not worry that you are alone and that you have no money. We are with you and our power goes with you. Do not entertain any doubts. Everything will happen at the appropriate time. People will learn of the miraculous benefits of devout austerity and the true worship of a dedicated yoga. This is the First Phase of your Program. Continue doing your duty. Do not think that our power is insignificant. You have less power but, when both of us unite, our power will be intensified, just as one and one make eleven. Moreover, this is a program being organized by a divine power. So why entertain any doubts? In due course all arrangements will be made. You need not worry about outlining any program at present. Go on with your studies, your performance of penance, and your fight for freedom. Live for the time being at your place of birth and fulfill these three parts of your first Phase.

"I can also give you a hint of the future plan. Your tasks of publishing ancient literature and of building a large religious organization are to be accomplished while living in Mathura. Completion of your ceremonies of penance will also be performed there. Publishing your books and performing your other activities relating to ascent of divinity in man and descent of Heaven on Earth will also be accomplished in their proper order at Mathura. These achievements will be a unique achievement in all of history.

"The third phase is to fulfill the desire of all these Rushis who live in astral bodies. You have to sow the seeds of Rushi traditions, which will spread world-wide in their own way. This work will have to be done at the site where seven Rushis performed penance, in Hardwar [the present site of Shanti Kunj]. Each of these things will be done properly in its respective place. At present, I have given you only a hint. In due course, you will be summoned and receive a detailed outline. You will be summoned three times for three purposes.

"In addition, you will also have a fourth burden to shoulder in the last part of the century. Then you will have to shoulder the most difficult and far-reaching task to help solve the extremely intricate problems pervading this entire universe. It is no use discussing it yet. You will know, at the proper time, what to do and it will be accomplished."

I had heard that holy yogis with supernatural powers lived in the caves of the Himalayas, and that by merely seeing one, a man can feel accomplished and gratified. In my journey, I found no basis to the rumor. Without my having to express it, Gurudev read my thoughts. He kept his hand on my shoulder and asked, "Do you feel that you need a holy man with supernatural powers? Are you not satisfied with having a glimpse of the astral bodies of the Rushis? Are you not satisfied knowing me?"

It was not a matter of lack of confidence, but merely curiosity. Again Gurudev read my thoughts and said, lightly, "There are such yogis, no doubt; but there are two new considerations. Lately, improvements in communications and transportation have increased the number of tourists and visitors here. This hinders the performance of yog [the working hard at a special task to accomplish a specific goal]. Moreover, if the yogis had tried to move to another place, it would be difficult to fulfill their physical needs. Therefore, all these Saints have abandoned their physical form to live in their astral bodies. They have even changed their way of performing yog. Moreover, since most of the pilgrims who come are not competent, worthy holy men, why should the Rushis appear before such undeserving people, shower them with gifts, and so waste their powers? In short, it is not possible for anyone to have seen such sages. Nevertheless, the next time that you come to the Himalayas, you will glimpse of such yogis with supernatural powers."

When Gurudev had first appeared before me, in my room, to guide me, I had learned how godly souls, who are part and parcel of the Infinite God, live in astral bodies. Only my childish curiosity had wanted to see them in the flesh. I was fully satisfied seeing the Rushis in their astral bodies and by Gurudev's assurances that I would glimpse them during my next visit to the Himalayas.

"When I summon you again," Gurudev said, you will have to stay between six months and a year. Your body has now become fit for living in conditions which prevail here. You will have to come three times to strengthen and ripen all that you have learned here, in the Himalayas, and all arrangements will be made to fulfill the needs of your physical body so that you will be able to endure, patiently, your move from the physical body into the astral. The human body is afflicted by *hunger, thirst, cold, heat, sleeplessness, and fatigue. One can hardly learn to overcome its limitations living at home . . . It is, therefore, necessary to live in a wilderness, to fight hard and struggle against lust, anger, greed, illusion, pride, and jealousy. You cannot manage this living at home. You will have to live apart, in the solitude of the Himalayas, to practice the physical endurance and mental austerity and perform penance to fight internal limitations. By living three times for about three years in the Himalayas, and by establishing public contacts in your region during the rest of the time, we will see whether your training has become matured.*

This program was outlined by the godly soul of Gurudev, but was one to my liking. It fulfilled my own desire. I was fully convinced that by associating with pious persons and by regular study and meditation, I could learn to restrain the ten organs of senses of actions and the invisible mind man can get rid of disintegration and infirmities and his internal power can be awakened. This is the road to becoming a yogi with one who acquires supernatural powers, even while living in this physical life. Restraining the senses, eschewing material wealth, making the best use of your time, and disciplining your thoughts--these are four kinds of self-control. If these are fully regulated and controlled, a man gets liberated from lust, anger, greed, and attachment, and he becomes a superman and acquires supernatural power.

I wanted to immerse myself only in penance of yoga. But how could I do that? One who had dedicated himself had no choice of his own. Therefore, when I heard from the mouth of Gurudev what I was required to do, I was too happy to contain myself, and started waiting anxiously for the proper time.

Gurudev announced, "Our talks are over now. Go to Gangotri, where arrangements have been made for your stay. Start your yoga at Bhagirath Shila [the rock where King Bhagirath once performed penance]. After one year of this, return home. I will be looking after you regularly."

With that, Gurudev disappeared. His messenger left me at Gomukh, and from there I reached the place he had indicated. After my year, I returned home. This time, I did not face the difficulties which had dogged my every step on my journey out, for I had now passed my tests. What difficulties could remain for my return journey?

When I reached home, I had gained eighteen pounds and my face had become red and round. My vitality had increased considerably. I was always jovial.

In fact, that pilgrimage was an important turning point in my life. The very first sight of the normally imperceptible divine Rushis who controlled and organized matters relating to the affairs of this universe left an indelible imprint on my inner self. I also had an inkling on this journey about my goal in life, my future course, and about the concerned spiritual souls who were to act as my colleagues. My first visit to the Himalayas was an experience which could inspire other people.

Chapter 6

A Soldier For Independence

Soon another test came. Mahatma Gandhi and his followers struggled for the independence of India. Gandhi's Congress Party urged "Satyagrah" or non-cooperation with the British authorities. They urged people to mass in the streets, face the threat of British bullets, and go to jail to achieve independence. Shree Ram joined this movement.

His conscience told him that this historic opportunity should not be wasted. He should leave his comfortable home, his wealthy family, and volunteer for a freedom march.

Rumors spread that participants in the non-cooperation movement would be either shot dead or sentenced to life imprisonment. Family members, relatives and friends pleaded with those they knew to forsake the movement. Shree Ram's family pleaded with him.

"It will be an act of suicide," they pleaded.

"It will be an act of conscience," he replied.

"We will fast until we die if you go," some told him.

"I will disinherit you," his mother threatened.

"You will no longer be considered part of our family," his brothers said. "We may even have you kidnapped by the dacoit, the hired thugs, if you don't forget the movement."

Shree Ram listened calmly. Where did his responsibility lie? Was his nation's need greater than his family's? Would awakening a nation's consciousness justify defying his family? From where could he get wise judgment?

From yourself, his soul told him. Shree Ram joined the fight for independence.

His family responded by locking him in his room. He knocked upon the locked door and pleaded, but nobody would open it. Finally, he hit upon an idea.

He removed his shirt and dhoti, a traditional Indian garment, and stood in only his underwear.

"Mummy," he shouted through the walls, "open the door quickly. I have to use the toilet." His mother looked through the window, saw him in his underwear, and believed him. She opened the door, and he bolted through, down the hall, out the door and up the road, 18 miles, at night, barefoot on a road covered with stones, thorns and shrubs.

He reached the Congress tent in Agra and enrolled himself as a soldier for independence.

On one protest march, the leaders selected Shree Ram to lead the way, holding the national flag in his hands.

Ahead stood a contingent of British police. At an officer's signal, the police charged, swinging their clubs, thrashing the unarmed marchers. The line broke; the marchers scattered--but Shree Ram, with the flag upright, marched on.

Police tried to snatch the flag from his hands, and, when he would not surrender it, tried to beat it from him. Shree Ram held on, with the flag between his teeth. They thrashed him into unconsciousness. When he came to, friends pulled the torn remnants of the flag from his mouth.

Shree Ram prays six hours a day. He spends at least two hours reading. He averages about 80 pages a day; about 2400 pages a month; 28,800 pages a year. He has read about 1.73 million pages in 60 years.

He reads, not for entertainment, but as though reading for his Ph.D. He remembers all that he reads. In a discussion with those around him, he seems like a "moving encyclopedia."

During the struggle for independence, he spent many periods in jail. There he improved his English by reading the newspaper, *Leader*. Sometimes he asked friends for help in reading and writing, with only a sheet of metal to write on and only stones for chalk. In exchange, he taught them Sanskrit and other Indian language. He wrote more than 300 poems while in jail.

Shree Ram learned many lessons from the independence movement that he would apply in the future.

In 1933 a Congress convened in Calcutta. The authorities warned that whoever attended would either be shot or imprisoned. Madanmohan Malaviyaji, a leader in the fight for freedom; Devidas, Mahatma Gandhi's son; Jawaharlal Nehru; and Mata Swaruprani were among those imprisoned. So was Shree Ram.

One day, while in jail, Shree Malaviyaji made a speech, exhorting greater support for the movement. "Each man should contribute one paisa [a unit of Indian currency]," he cried, "and each woman a fist of grain. This way, each Indian will feel that Congress belongs to them!"

Later, Shree Ram would adopt this idea to raise money for his own followers and to encourage cooperation among them. Today, many people donate twenty paisa daily to help realize Shree Ram's goals.

Meanwhile, still in jail, Shree Ram performed the work assigned to him efficiently and smoothly. Soon, his jailers made him the head worker among the freedom fighters.

The leaders of the Congress party also noticed his honesty, his dedication to work, and his great faith in their goals. They sought his leadership in the movement.

To document their protest to the British "Farmers' Tax," the Party leaders asked Shree Ram to survey every farmer of the Agra District. He completed the survey in a matter of days and submitted his report to the Congress.

"How'd he bloody-well do it?" top British officials asked. "It would have taken us months. Even our civil service couldn't have done this well."

Shree Ram had learned to perform several tasks simultaneously.

Chapter 7

The Second Phase of Journey and Assessment of the Field of Work

Written by Shree Ram Sharma Acharya and translated by Shree Satyanarayan Pandya.

A period of about ten years had passed since I was summoned to the Himalayas to appear in the first test. It was not considered necessary to call me in between this time. I used to see Gurudev in the same pose in which I had seen him for the first time and he used to express his approval. Never did I feel that I was alone. Throughout these ten years, I felt that he was always with me.

The struggle for freedom was going on. The weather was fine. I again received a message to reach the Himalayas. The orders could not be ignored. I informed my family members and started on the journey the very next day. The road still went up to Uttar-kashi only. Road construction work was going on at that time beyond Uttar-kashi.

The route was known to me. The weather was not so cold as it was last time. The halting places were not desolate because pilgrims were coming and going. I found no difficulty this time. I had comparatively less luggage with me. Although I was not feeling as comfortable as at home, the journey on the whole was not intolerable.

I was not put to any test to which I was subjected last time. The way up to Gangotri was such that it was not necessary to make any query. Only, the track of fourteen miles from Gangotri to Gomukh changed every year due to melting of snow and breaking and falling of rocks. Small rivulets also changed sometimes their course on account of falling of rocks. This route can be crossed by seeking guidance of some local persons or by using one's own sharp intellect. In this manner, I reached Gomukh.

I had to cover rest of the journey with Gurudev's messenger. He was a shadowy person and was in astral body. Gurudev used to take different work from him from time to time. Whenever I visited the Himalayas, he was in charge of taking me up to Nandanvan and back down to Gomukh. With his help, I arrived in less time. We did not talk to each other en route.

As soon as I reached Nandanvan I saw Gurudev before me in his astral body. My sentiments and joy knew no bounds. My lips started trembling and nose became wet. It appeared as if some deficiency of some lost part of my own body has been fulfilled. As a symbol of his deep love for me, he put his hand on my head. The formality of adoration and blessings was thus completed. Gurudev hinted to me about going to see the Rushis again for seeking guidance. I was overwhelmed.

Almost all the Rushis of Satyug live in this region of the inaccessible Himalayas in astral bodies. I had

*met them here earlier. Although they do not need any
specific place or object, they have each for their
convenience reserved a specific cave.*

*In my first visit, I could simply bow before them
and receive their blessings indirectly. This time I had
the privilege to listen to their messages. Gurudev took
and introduced me to each one of them. They appeared
to be as mass of light. But when I transformed my
subtle body I could see them in bodies in which they
lived in Satyug. They were in the same form in which
worldly people see them in their imagination.
Necessary formalities were observed. I kept my head
on their feet. They touched my head. I was thrilled and
was overwhelmed with joy.*

*Coming to the main purpose, they said by
inspiration speech or astral language that the
activities which they used to launch when they lived in
their physical bodies had almost come to an end. What
remained was nothing but their ruins. They said that
they were much pained when by their divine insight
they saw the present conditions. The entire region
from Hardwar to Gangotri was the region of Rushis in
which they used to remain engrossed in Penance.
There were several hermitages here and there on the
lines of Hermitage of Rushi Jamadagni at Uttar-kashi.
All Rushis were engaged in their own research work,
penance, and yoga. Gods used to live where the Rushis
lived at present. After the Ice Age everything has
changed and the activities of the Rushis have almost
come to an end.*

*The Rushi said that some temples have, no doubt,
been built here and there in Uttarkhand so that
offerings in the form of money could be made to deities*

*and caretakers of temples may earn their livelihood.
But nobody asks or gives an indication who the Rushis
were, where they were, and what they did. Thus,
Rushi traditions have almost come to an end.*

*All the Rushis to whom I was introduced
repeated almost the same story. While bidding
farewell, there were tears in their eyes. It appeared as
if all of them were sad and afflicted with sorrow. What
could I say? How could I do the work which so many
Rushis used to do? I had no strength to do so. I was
moved when I saw them with heavy hearts. I thought,
if God had made me capable enough, I would not have
remained mute. But I returned speechless after seeing
the Rushis. Silence overtook me. I was stupefied.
There were tears in my eyes. It pained me like a sting
of scorpion to see so many great and most capable
Rushis, so unhappy, helpless, and worried.*

*Gurudev's soul and my soul were moving
together. We were looking at each other. His face was
also sad. Oh God! What an odd time has come that no
successor of these Rushis has been born? Their lineage
has come to an end. Not a single activity which was
initiated by the Rushis is alive at present. There are
hundreds of millions of brahmans and millions of (so-
called) saints. If amongst them there had been only ten
or twenty truly living persons they would have
performed marvelously like Buddha and Gandhi.*

*I recalled that in the past when the princess shed
tears and asked, "Who will revive the Vedas?"
Kumaril Bhatt appeared and said, "Please do not
lament so long as Kumaril is alive on earth." Kumaril
Bhatt did what he undertook to do. But today there is
neither brahman nor saint, and a Rushi is almost out*

of the question. Only hypocrites are seen today screaming everywhere like a wolf in lamb's disguise. All such ideas arose in my mind for the whole day after I had returned to my cave. Gurudev was reading my mind. He, too, was unhappy like me.

Gurudev said, "Then do one thing. We again go to meet all the Rushis. Tell them, if you so direct, I may sow the seed but you will have to do manuring and watering so that the crop may grow. At least by making such an effort you will feel much relieved. Also ask them how to make a beginning and what will be its outline. Tell them, 'I will definitely do something. If all of you are kind enough to shower your grace, there is bound to be greenery in this dry graveyard'."

Whatever may happen, I could even say that on Gurudev's command I am prepared to jump in the fire and die. Gurudev could read my mind. This time, I saw his face blooming with pleasure like supreme Divine Lotus. Both of us were quiet but happy. We decided to return back again and meet all the Rushis whom we had met last night. When they saw us again, each one of them expressed satisfaction as well as amazement.

I stood spell-bound with folded hands and my head bowed down before them. Gurudev conveyed my aspiration, desire and zeal to them indirectly in astral language and said, "He is not lifeless. He will do whatever he says. Kindly indicate how the seed of the work left by you has to be sown. If manuring, watering, etc. is done by us, his efforts will not go to waste."

Thereafter, Gurudev invited them all to kindly attend in astral bodies, the 1008 Gayatri yagna which was to be performed at Mathura on the completion of Gayatri puruscharans and said that he is a monkey although Hanuman, a bear although Jamvant, a vulture although Jatayu.[1] Kindly direct him and entertain the hope that what has been left out will be rebuilt and the off-shoot will transform into a huge tree. He said, "Why should we be disappointed? Why should we not expect things from him when he had with great devotion discharged responsibilities which were entrusted to him during his past births?"

This talk was going on with one of the Rushis but hardly did it take a moment for this invitation to reach them and they all gathered. Disappointment disappeared, hope revived, and a future programme was chalked out: that a seed of that which we all do be sown in a field, a seedling be prepared in the nursery, and when these plants are planted everywhere, there will be blooming gardens everywhere.

This was the scheme of building Shanti-kunj which was to be undertaken after conclusion of my stay at Mathura. The scheme of building Gayatri Nagar-Shanti Kunj and raising the structure of Brahmavarchas Research Institute was also explained in detail. Each and every word which I was told was engraved on my mental canvas and I decided that soon after completion of twenty four Gayatri

---

[1]Hanuman and Jamvant - Devotees of Lord Shree Ram who helped Shree Ram in the war against King Ravan of Shri Lanka.

Jatayu - Fought with King Ravan who was returning to Shri Lanka with kidnapped Sita, wife of Lord Shree Ram.

purushcharan of 2.4 million, I will prepare an outline of this work. It is impossible that a person who is recipient of Gurudev's protection and patronage may ever be unsuccessful.

I stayed for a day more. Explaining in detail about the completion of puruscharan, Gurudev said, "I have been studying all the past events minutely and rectifying anything which was found to be improper. I called you this time to explain what is to be done in the future. There is not much time now left for completion of your puruscharan. Go to Mathura, complete it and start the second phase of your life from Mathura.

"Next to Prayag, Mathura is a central place in the country. It is convenient from the point of view of communication. After independence, your political responsibility will be over but your work will not be complete. Political revolution is bound to come there. Government will look after the economic revolution and other allied matters but three more revolutions will have to be initiated through the agency of religious institutions. The country became dependent and weak not because there was shortage of brave persons who could defeat the aggressors. Internal weaknesses are responsible for downfall and degeneration of the country. Others have only taken advantage of this weakness.

"Moral, intellectual, and social revolutions are to be accomplished. For this, it is necessary to collect appropriate persons and express views about the work which has to be done. So leave your village and go to Mathura, take a small house there and publish a monthly magazine and also publish matters relating to these three kinds of revolutions. In due course, you

have to build a grand Gayatri temple near Mathura in the land where Durvasa Rushi of Satyug had performed penance and make arrangements for the stay, residence, etc. of your colleagues. Then you have to perform a 1008 yagna after the completion of twenty-four mahapuruscharans by way of completion. It has always been the tradition in Purushcharan to perform yagna along with the recital of spells. After completion of twenty-four Purushcharan each of 2.4 million recital of spells you have to celebrate a 1008 yagna and offer 2.4 million times different herbs with ghee. On that occasion a huge organization will be evolved which will initiate the work of public awakening through the agency of religious institutions. This is the first phase of the completion of Mahapuruscharan. After discharging this responsibility for about twenty-five years, you have to go to Sapt-Sarovar, Hardwar, live there and complete the work of revival of Rushi traditions for which you have given your consent to the Rushis."

Gurudev explained in detail how work at Mathura was to be done. He also indicated the outline of the work of translation of ancient scriptures, their publication and publicity and setting up organization of branches.

I had assured Gurudev in my very first meeting with him that nothing will be left undone to fulfill his directions. But there was only one doubt in my mind. How the need of money and manpower will be fulfilled for the accomplishment of so huge a task? Gurudev read my mind, laughed and said, "Do not worry about these material resources. Start sowing whatever you possess. Its harvest will be hundred times. All the

work which has been entrusted to you will be fulfilled."
Gurudev himself indicated what I possess, how and
when it has to be sown, and how and when it was to
yield harvest.

I kept everything which Gurudev said firmly in
my mind. there was no question of forgetting it. How
can a soldier forget the command of a General? I could
not neglect or disregard what I was told to do.

Our talks concluded. This time I was directed to
stay in the Himalayas only for six months. All
necessary arrangements were made where I had to
stay. Gurudev's assistant left me at Gomukh. I
reached the destination and completed six months
stay. When I reached home my health was much
better. My happiness and earnestness had increased.
It reflected on my face. People said that it appears that
there was some place of happiness and comfort in the
Himalayas where you go and come back much
healthier every time. I simply laughed and did not give
any reply.

Chapter 8

In Mathura

Shree Ram went once to Mathura, just to see the city. At the time he knew no one there.

Some years later upon orders of his Gurudev, he returned there to rent a house in which to live and publish a monthly magazine.

Even in those days it was difficult to find a house. Finally, after a very long search, he located a house at Ghiyamandi which had been vacant for a long time. He inquired about the rent from the elderly woman who owned it.

"Fifteen Rupees," she said and handed him the keys.

The house had fifteen rooms, and although it was old, one rupee per room made it more than reasonable. Besides, Shree Ram liked the house. He gave a month's rent in advance, and the old woman smiled.

He moved in with his wife and children. The whole neighborhood started gossiping.

"Why?" asked Shree Ram.

Because the house is haunted, his new neighbors replied. Everyone who has stayed in the house has lost their life. You have been cheated because you are a stranger. If you stay after learning this, you, too, will suffer.

Shree Ram discounted the neighbors' remarks. It was difficult to get such a large house for so little rent. However, perhaps the house was haunted: All the first night a terrible commotion came from the top floor-- crying, laughing and fighting.

The house had no electricity. Shree Ram lit a lamp and slowly climbed to the top floor.

There he saw apparitions of men and women running away from him.

For ten nights, the same commotion recurred. Finally Shree Ram again climbed to the top floor, about 1 a.m., with his lamp in his hand.

"Stop!" he called at the running figures. "After all, you have been here a long time. You can all stay in the seven rooms of the top floor, and I will use the eight rooms downstairs. This way we can compromise: you don't get disturbed, nor do I have to suffer."

No answer came, but he had quiet from then on.

In 1937, Shree Ram began publishing a monthly magazine from this house. He named it *Akhand Jyoti, The Continuous Lamp*. It has no news and carries no advertising. He writes all the articles himself. Through it, Shree Ram communicates with the outside world. *Akhand Jyoti* has become like a lighthouse, enlightening the souls of thousands, offering a new direction to their lives.

Shree Ram revolutionized popular literature by translating the ancient Sanskrit classics into the language of laymen. Four Vedas, eighteen Puran, twenty-four Gita, six Darshan, *The Upanishad*, and other famous works appeared in its pages.

As his readership grew, Shree Ram expanded his list of publications. Eventually he wrote 200 books on the Art of Living, 100 biographies, numerous children's stories, treatises on social injustice, books on improving society, on science, and on religion. All told, he has written over 1,000 books. His 18,000 page *Encyclopedia of Gita* currently awaits publication.

When Dr. Radhakrishna Menon, the former President of India, read some of Shree Ram's works, he said, "If I had read these books years ago, I would have joined a religious institution instead of going into politics." Shortly thereafter, Shree Ram was honored with the title "Vedmurti Taponishth," or "Expert in Vedas and Practitioner of Strict Penance."

Shree Ram has received many honors, academic and otherwise. In 1933 the Indian Homeopathic Society of Medicine of Mahuva-Gujarat State awarded him both Doctor of Homeopathic Medicine and Doctor of Ayurvedic Medicine degrees. The same year, they honored him with the title Hakim-ul-Mulk. In 1939, Aligadh University granted him licenses as Doctor of Electropathy and Natureopathy Practice, and the University of Lahore bestowed their Doctor of Literature, with a medal of Hindi Literature, and Doctor in Psychology degrees upon him.

Eventually, Shree Ram's increased work load required expanded facilities. To begin with, he needed a quiet place to work. He chose a place situated on Vindravan Road, two kilometers from the City of Mathura on the banks of the Yamuna River. In 1952 he planned a Yagna ceremony on that spot and laid the corner stone for his Foundation, the Gayatri Tapobhumi.

Charity begins at home; and, just as light shines down from the top, so he who would lead any great movement must set the best example. So Shree Ram sold all the land that he had in his home village, except for a plot that he donated for a school.

Then he and his wife together mortgaged her jewelry to construct a building called Gayatri Tapobhumi.

Shree Ram donated all of his own personal belongings--his jewelry, books, land, even his printing presses--to God and called himself a "non-accepting" Brahmin, one who keeps nothing for himself.

Shree Ram placed an idol of the Goddess Gayatri in the temple at Gayatri Tapobhumi and began a holy fast and performed the yagna ceremony. For 24 days, from May 30 to June 22, 1953, he abstained from food, drinking only water from the River Ganges. All the while, he continued to work his daily routine although he lost 22 pounds in doing so. To light the Holy Fire of the Yagna, he used the sun.

Then he called for a Narmeg Yagna ceremony, a life-long pledge and, at that ceremony, 27 of his followers pledged their entire life's work to the fulfillment of Shree Ram's "revolution". Shree Ram vowed at the same Yagna that he would establish 1,250 libraries.

The Rushis of Himalaya had ordered Shree Ram to perform 1,008 Yagna to hasten to dawn of the new era.

So he marked off an area of seven square miles and erected 5,000 tents.

Shree Ram undertook to perform this Yagna virtually alone, between November 23, and November 29, 1958. His followers whispered, "What has he done? It takes over a thousand people, working together, to

make a Yagna. Never in all history has one person
tried to do so much alone."

He sent invitations to thousands of people; yet,
somehow, tens of thousands received invitations and
over 900,000 people came. As he always seemed to do,
Shree Ram drew to himself people who needed to be
awakened, so that the good that they had performed in
their previous lives did not remain dormant within.

Many pickpockets and would-be burglars also
came, yet not one thing got stolen. Something seemed
to have affected even the greediest of minds.

During the ceremony not one person got sick.

Throughout these four days, Shree Ram and his
wife fasted, eating nothing and drinking only water
from the Ganges. From morning to evening, they met
with people who had come especially to see them.

Shree Maganlal Gandhi, a friend of the author,
had once been "made alive again" by Shree Ram. Here,
he took charge of the grain that the congregation
would need to make food. Volunteer workers stored the
little bit of donated grain in a locked room, and only
Maganlal had the keys.

"Remove only what is needed," Shree Ram had
instructed him, "and re-lock the room as soon as the
grain is removed."

And that was another miracle--for four days, all
were fed, whatever the participants needed, the little
room supplied, and when the Yagna ended, 20,000
pounds of grain remained.

"Distribute the rest among the poor," Shree Ram
ordered.

Shree Ram, himself, kept the tiny money box. Yet
he continually drew out, as their needs required, until

millions of rupees had flowed from the box. As the crowds dispersed, it, too, had some left over.

Meanwhile, the 1,008 Yagnas had gone beautifully. A thousand participants united to form one. These newly awakened souls would now play an important role in creating the new era.

In addition, all of the Rushis that Shree Ram had seen on Himalaya came in their astral bodies, to this Yagna. Other mysterious things that happened will become apparent after Shree Ram's death.

The Saints and Rushis view the pain of others as if it were their own pain. Since there seems no end to the enmity, affliction, and grief abroad in the world today, their torture runs deep. Their primary concern remains how to make the world happier and to teach people to love in peace and free from pain. Shree Ram described his own self-induced torment in his Hindi-language book, *Sumsam ke Sahcher*.

Once a well-wisher suggested to Shreemati Bagwati Devi, Shree Ram's wife, that, as the jewel of his nation, Shree Ram should be provided with nutritious food. Shreemati Bagwati Devi, whom friends know as Mataji, agreed and offered her husband a full glass of orange juice.

"What is in the glass," he asked.

"The juice of an orange, for you," she replied.

He did not respond, but became very serious. His eyes filled with tears. He seemed to be suffocating. Had she done something wrong?

"We live in a country so economically poor," he replied, that millions for whom I have a heart-felt affection have not enough food for one day at a time.

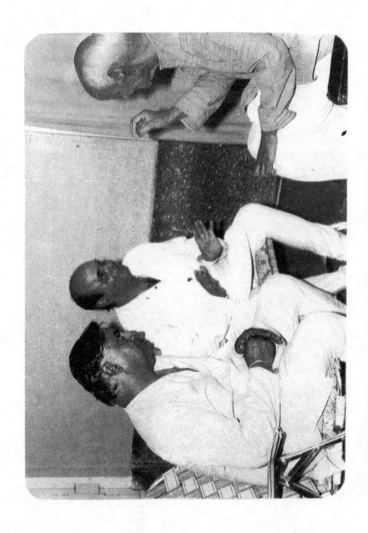

PRODUCER AND DIRECTOR OF TV SERIES RAMAYAN,
RAMANAND SAGAR AND HIS SON SUBHASH WITH SHREE RAM SHARMA

How can I accept the juice that the others in our organization cannot have?

"My mission is not restricted to my own physical fitness, but to the total well-being of all volunteers of Gayatri Tapobhumi. So many are young or old or weak; they need more nutrition than I. What I am unable to provide for all members of my organization, I have no right to.

"Of course it is good that I have nutritious food. It is equally as good that others have it. To have it exclusively seems selfish. Even should it help my body, it would hurt my consciousness."

Shree Ram's consciousness reaches out to all animals and human. In Mathura, many eyes have witnessed a sparrow, mouse, or squirrel at lunch across the clearing from where he sits. Once a mouse scurried onto his plate and sat on his chopati (a type of thin bread). As Shree Ram lifted the chopati into the air, the mouse clung to it, until their eyes met. "Guruji" sees himself, and his own soul, in every being.

It is written in the ancient text *Kalkipuran* that management of Mathura will be given to Suryaketu and he will then move to north of Mathura.

In 1971, Shree Ram left Mathura for Hardwar and passed responsibility to Lilaputi Sharma (Suryaketu).

ॐ भूर्भुवः स्वः तत्सवितुर्वरेण्यं भर्गोदेवस्य
धीमहि धियो योनः प्रचोदयात्।

SHREE GODDESS GAYATRI
(ONE IMAGINATION)

Chapter 9

The Great Gayatri Mantra

Oam Bhoor Bhuvah Swah Tat Savitur
Varenyam Bhargo Devasya Dheemahi
Dhio Yo Nah Prachodayat

Oam	Almighty God
Bhoor	Embodiment of Vital or Spiritual Energy
Bhuvah	Destroyer of Suffering
Swah	Embodiment of Happiness
tat	that
Savitur	bright, luminious, like the sun
Varenyam	best
Bhargo	Destroyer of Sins
Devasya	Divine
dheemahi	may receive
dhiyo	intellect
Yo	Who
naha	our
prachodayat	may inspire

O God, Thou art the Giver of Life, the Remover of pains
and Sorrows, the Bestower of Happiness;
O Creator of the Universe,
May we receive Thy supreme, sin-destroying light;
May Thou guide our intellect in the right direction.

Misconceptions abound, in the Western world, about the many Hindu "gods" and "goddesses." The one, omnipotent Creator of the Universe--GOD--is, of course, formless. However one of God's manifestations may be that of *Sakar*: the shape of a human being. A worshipper might shape the form and nature of a visualization to conform to his or her belief or need, but we must keep in mind that the visualization, that image, is imaginary and not real. God is One and does not have a different face for each sect. The purpose of a Hindu image of a manifestation of God serves, as in the Christian Church, to help the worshipper understand, visualize, and assimilate the invisible God through the medium of visible symbols.

In the Indian language, the Divine Power [*Shakti*] that has created all things is a feminine word. In India that Creator, the one God worshipped by all civilized people of the world, is called the Goddess Gayatri.

Vice fosters of all the evil committed throughout the world. To obliterate vice, we should pray for and seek to acquire only true knowledge, which comes from God, through worship of Gayatri. As it smothers evil, worship of Gayatri inspires us to do noble deeds. These noble deeds power the advancement of mankind, and from them man derives happiness, peace and a sense of worth of self.

Whatever their outward differences, all sects of Hinduism accept the worship of Gayatri as the panacea for our ills and the driving force behind man's salvation. The philosophers of this century, who claim that their wisdom springs from no divine source, give the greatest credit to logic. Still, Gayatri could prove the most valuable spiritual instrument man has to ensure his own deliverance from the rancors of earthly life and to escape the otherwise endless cycle of rebirths and deaths.

True religion and true science do not contradict each other but play supporting roles in the growth of each individual and of mankind. Dr. Harold Caselinge of the University of Pennsylvania published a paper documenting his research conclusions that most successful human beings manage to fuse their spiritual and scientific elements.

For one thing, our spiritual side can channel our applications of science away from destruction towards creation. Earlier in this century, science proceeded as if the physical element were supreme. Now men of science realize that all objects are perishable and that all matter is ultimately transmutable into energy. This support Vedic philosophy, for during recitation of the Gayatri Mantra, each sound of the Mantra creates vibrations in a specific energy center, called a gland, in your body, as surely as striking a typewriter key prints a specific letter on your paper.

It is said that the Gayatri Mantra spells should be pronounced correctly and the worship performed in a prescribed manner. However, although millions perform the mantra daily, and although millions have done so for thousands of years, there is not a single recorded instance of anyone who came to harm for performing the ceremony incorrectly. The great Rushis agree that the goddess Gayatri is a kind, noble, generous, and compassionate Mother, ever concerned for her children's welfare. Even as a worldly mother harbors no malice for a child who behaves wrongly, so the Mother of the Universe showers kindness on her family. Omissions or errors in the performance of her ritual flow away in Her divine stream of love and affection.

For instance, Shri Bhukhandas Laxman Khatri worked all his life as a tailor in Bombay. When his children were grown and moved out on their own, Shri Bhukhandas retired to the "country". He moved into a dwelling not far from my home. One day we fell to discussing the Gayatri Mantra, which we both recited daily.

"But you are pronouncing it wrong," he told me, "It should be 'Oam Bhu Bhuravaha . . . ' I should know; I was taught by a Brahmin."

"But you are wrong," I corrected. "It should be 'Oam Bhur Bhuvah . . . ' And I should know, for I learned from a scholar of the Veda, Shree Ram Sharma Acharya, who performed penance for 24 years!"

So we consulted the teacher of Sanskrit at our local school, who confirmed my pronunciation.

Had any harm befallen my new neighbor for his mispronunciation? Had Gayatri withheld her favors?

"No," he replied frankly. "She has made me happy ever since I began to say the Mantra."

Scientists know that a singer who hits high "C" can shatter a crystal wine glass. What we perceive as "sound" consists of vibrations travelling through the air; as these vibrations strike the glass, its molecules being to vibrate at the same frequency as the sound waves that engulf it until it shatters.

Modern researchers have recorded sound waves emitted by people reciting the Gayatri Mantra. These

THE TEN PRINCIPAL INCARNATION (AVATAR) OF THE HINDUS

(1)　　The Matsya - Avatar

(2)　　The Kurmma - Avatar

(3)　　The Varah - Avatar

(4)　　The Narshia - Avatar

(5)　　The Vaman - Avatar

(6)　　The Parshuram - Avatar
　　　　(Swami Sarveshwaranandji)

(7)　　The Rama - Avatar

(8)　　The Krishna - Avatar

(9)　　The Buddh - Avatar

(10)　　The Kalki - Avatar
　　　　(Shree Ram Sharma Acharya)

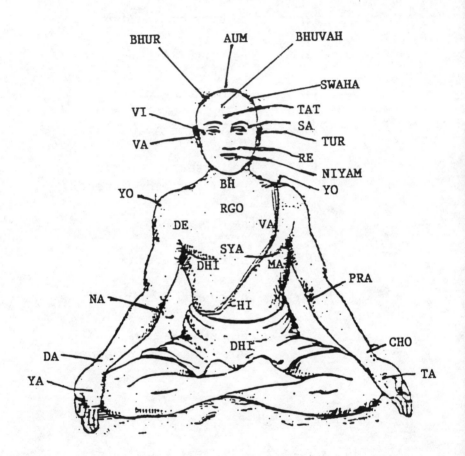

sound waves set up measurable responses in specific centers of the human body.

As our stomachs respond to food, so our spiritual centers, our glands, respond to sound. The twenty-four sounds of the Sanskrit Gayatri Mantra activate, in proper sequence, a thread of spiritual glands and arteries.

The illustration on the facing page shows the relation of the sounds of the Gayatri Mantra to specific centers of the body.

The chart below diagrams the relationship.

Letter	Gland	Power
tat	tapini	success
sa	success	bravery
vi	Vishva	maintenance
tur	tushti	welfare
va	varda	yog
re	revati	love
ni	sooksma	money, wealth
yam	gyan	brilliance
bhar	bharg	difference
go	gomati	intellect
de	devika	subjugation
va	varahi	devotion
sya	sinhani	determination
dhee	dhyan	life-force
ma	maryada	self-restraint
li	sfula	penance
dhi	medha	farsightedness
yo	yogmaya	awakening
yo	yogini	production
naha	dharini	sweetness

pra	prabhav	ideal
cho	ooshma	courage
da	drashya	wisdom
yat	niranjan	unselfishness

Utterance of these sounds, combined into the Gayatri Mantra stimulates the nerve fibers and glands of the body. Just as in a negative way the sound of chalk squeaking on a blackboard sends chills down our spines, so in a positive, soothing way the Gayatri Mantra stores a particular power in each of our biological centers. These specific twenty-four attributes are so essential to human growth and development that spiritual and material success, achievement, and prosperity soon shower upon the devotee. Most worshippers attribute their progress to the beneficence of some God or Goddess. In truth, these sounds create a subtle transformation inside of each of us through a process scientifically planned by sages of Gayatri worship.

Thus the worship of Gayatri is more than blind faith. It is a scientific act that yields many benefits.

Eastern Wise Men compare the Gayatri Mantra to the Elixir of Life:

> *The Japas of Gayatri, performed with a balanced mind and a true heart, are capable of removing all kinds of calamities and difficulties in bad times, and they become very useful tools for the progress of the soul, as it reaches towards salvation.*
>
> *--Mahatma Gandhi*

Gayatri brings people who have gone astray back to the right path.

--Lokamanya Tilak

The worship of Gayatri brings godly light to our souls; as a result, we become free from worldly ties and physical wants.

--Madan Mohan Malaviya

The main organ of yoga is worship of Gayatri.

--T. Subba Rao

If any hymn can awaken India, it is the Gayatri Mantra.

--Rabindranath Tagore

Gayatri on the one hand, and all the Vedas with their six branches in another, were weighed in a scale, and the pan in which Gayatri was placed was found to be heavier. The Upanishadas are the kernel of Vedas and Gayatri with "vaayahritis" is the essence of The Upanishadas. Gayatri is the Mother of Vedas, destroyer of all sins. There is no other Mantra either in Heaven or on Earth more purifying than Gayatri.

--Ancient Sage Yogiraj Yagnavalkya

A devotee becomes liberated by Gayatri recitation alone, even if he does not do any other devotional practice. He gets the virtues of this world, as well as of the other. Ten thousand repetitions will save a man from any difficulty.

--Ancient Sage Shaunik

Gayatri is a highly purifying Mantra, and it is potent enough to remove all vices and frailties. One who understand the essence of Gayatri Mantra in a proper way enjoys all the happiness of this world.
                    --Ancient Sage Atri

Just as honey is the essence of flowers, Ghee is the essence of milk, so Gayatri is the essence of Vedas. Gayatri is a Kamdhenu (celestial cow) to him who has accomplished it in full.
          --Ancient Sage Maharshi Vyash

A dull-witted, licentious, or unbalanced person can be elevated by the grace of Gayatri and he is sure to be liberated. One who worships Gayatri with purity and firmness of mind is sure to achieve self-realization.
              --Ancient Sage Vasisthji

The power of the soul increases by Gayatri Japas.
                  --Founder of Aarya
              Samaj Swami Dayanand

The Yagna enables people to fulfill their hearts' desires. It helps parents to beget a son, a bachelor to marry a beautiful bride, and a spinster to wed a handsome groom. It enables a person of goodwill to acquire divinity, but one performing it with no desire what-so-ever attains God.
          --Ancient epic Matsyapurana 93/117

*Those who want to have cattle,
children, freedom from anguish, and
fearlessness can have them by chanting
Gayatri Mantra regularly, with faith.*
                    --Ancient epic Gayatri Panchang-1

*Gayatri can keep a man from falling
into hell. There is nothing better than
Gayatri either in heaven or on earth. A
knower of Gayatri is sure to reach heaven.*
                              --Ancient Sage Shankha

*God invoked Gayatri Mantra of the
three vedas. There is not a single Mantra
more potent than Gayatri. Whoever
regularly does "Gayatri Jap" continually for
three years attains supreme godhood.*
                        --Ancient Sage Bhagwan Manu

*The Gayatri Mantra does not belong to
any particular sect of worship, nor is it
restricted to any certain community. It is
universal, for the whole world. It contains
in it the culture not of any particular society,
but the culture of humanity. The Gayatri
Mantra is a treasure and heritage that
belongs to the whole of humanity.*
                    *--Vedmurti, Taponistha, Brahmarshi
                        Shree Ram Sharma Acharya*

India became the most advanced society of
ancient times because it tapped the vast power of the
Gayatri Mantra. In previous ages, Saints, Munis, and
Rushis achieved efficacious, invaluable, divine power
through the Gayatri Mantra. It helps with every aspect
of life.

Many stories illustrate its power.

In the Atlantic Ocean lies a black hole called "The Bermuda Triangle." From the very mists of time, through to the present day, it has swallowed innumerable men and ships, even airplanes, that passed within its grip. In the early 1980's, a well-known Hollywood actor named Peter Sellers lost his way while flying his airplane and found himself trapped in the Bermuda Triangle. He had lost contact with the control tower, and his machine no longer responded to its controls. He thought that his plan must be trapped by some invisible power, fiercely drawn in that power's direction. He glanced at the altmeter; he was falling fast into the sea. The sea, approaching rapidly beneath him, somehow recalled a vision of a visit to India and a performer of yoga there who had taught him the Gayatri Mantra.

"Recite it whenever you are in difficulty," the Guru had advised. He was certainly in difficulty.

He began to recite the Gayatri Manta and, to his surprise, found himself instantly out of the trap of the Bermuda Triangle. He was saved.

The worshipper, by reciting the Gayatri Mantra, achieves Divine Power and frees him/herself from evil acts. This power incinerates any evil that attempts to penetrate its shield.

Shree Madhavacharya sought penance through the Gayatri Mantra for twelve years, but the goddess Gayatri did not seem to be pleased with him. Disillusioned, he stopped his recitation. Instead, he started to perform penance that would appeal to the Spirit Bal-Bhairav, who can be pleased very easily. Within six months, Shree Madhavacharya had pleased the Spirit who, however, would not present himself to Shree Madhavacharya's face.

Instead Bal-Bhairav appeared at the holy man's back and told him to ask for a boon.

Shree Madhavacharya opened his eyes, but saw nothing.

"It must have been an illusion," he thought, closed his eyes, and resumed his meditation for penance.

As soon as he did so, he again heard the voice, calling, "My child, what boon do you want?"

Again Shree Madhavacharya opened his eyes, but saw only the breeze wafting through the trees. He replied, "If you, Spirit, are pleased with me, then present yourself, physically, in front of me."

"But I am physically behind you," the Spirit replied. The Saint asked why.

"Because of the Divine Power of Gayatri," the Spirit answered. "If I try to appear before you, the Divine Power of Gayatri in your body will burn me into ashes. So while I stand behind thee, I will grant thee one boon."

"Then tell me why," asked Shree Madhavacharya, "after twelve years of doing the penance of Gayatri, is She not pleased with me?"

"Perform the penance for one more year," Spirit Bal-Bhairav replied, "and you will find Gayatri pleased.

So Shree Madhavacharya performed Gayatri's penance for twelve more months, and Gayatri was pleased and appeared before him.

"Why, Gayatri Mata [mother]," he asked, "why did it take so long to please you?"

Gayatri Mata showed him a vision of a mountain range on fire.

"In your previous life," she said, "you sinned by killing seven Brahmins. To expiate those sins required a long period of penance.

"These seven mountains represent the seven Brahmins that you killed, and until your sins were eradicated by penance, no Divine Being could appear before you."

Thereafter, Shree Madhavacharya received whatever he asked for from the Gayatri Mata.

Professors at the University of Hamburg, in West Germany, are now conducting research into the power of the Gayatri Mantra. In America, Howard Stangel researched the power of all known religious mantras on the basis of the power of sounds. He concluded that the Gayatri Mantra was the most powerful in the world, for it alone produced 110,000 sound waves per second.

Experiments by Dr. Charles Leadbeater of the Theosophical Society, established that uttering the Gayatri Mantra enables the worshipper to tap the power of the Sun, increasing his or her aura by 27 to 37 centimeters.

The communist author Arthur Cheisler once commented to R.K. Karanjia, editor of the *Blitz*, a weekly newspaper published in Bombay, "If all the inhabitants of India utter the great Gayatri Mantra simultaneously, there would be no need for India to make a nuclear bomb. The universal uttering of the Gayatri Mantra would create a vast power, like a sound bomb. It would automatically activate . . . the sound waves creating a shield of defense for protection. This shield can protect us from huge calamities."

A few years back, part of an American satellite was expected to fall back to Earth. NASA scientists calculated that it would fall on western India, somewhere between the small cities of Surat and Vadodra, destroying property and killing many inhabitants. To avert these calamities, Shree Ram Sharma asked his devotees to recite the great Gayatri Mantra at odd times during the night, particularly between 9:00 and 10:00 pm, instead of the customary early morning hours usually between midnight and 8:00 a.m. Although puzzled, the devotees did as Shree Ram bid. Miraculously, between 9:00 and 10:00 pm, the satellite fell into the deserts of Australia, injuring no living thing.

Recitation of the Gayatri Mantra seems to heighten one's psychic powers. The grandfather of my best friend, one of the ten most respected business leaders of his town, practiced the Gayatri Mantra faithfully. One morning, while reciting the Mantra, a vision predicted his death. Three days later, he died as the vision foretold. In a similar vision, Saint Kan Brahmachari foresaw his death, six months before it occurred.

Reciting the Gayatri Mantra can also increase one' memory power. Mahatma Anand Swami of Aray Samaj, a great devotee of this mantra, described his early life in one of his many books, *Anand Gayatri Katha*. As a child his memory was so poor that he could not remember his lessons. One day he was paddled by his teacher for his forgetfulness, and then again by his father for arriving home late from school.

"Furthermore," his father told him, "from now on, you are to deliver dinner to the sage Shree Nityanand Swamji."

Swamji soon noticed the boy's despair. After he had eaten, he called the boy to him.

"What bothers you," the elder asked, his voice quiet and full of sympathy.

Hearing the tone in Swamji's voice, the young boy began to cry.

"Sit on my lap," Swamji told the boy. "Now, tell me your problem."

My memory is so terrible, the boy replied, that I just can't remember my lessons. I try, but I can't remember.

So Swamji wrote the words to the Gayatri Mantra on a piece of paper and explained their meaning. "Now recite these daily," he said. "Begin between 2:00 and 3:00 a.m., while the rest of your family still sleeps."

The future Mahatma Anand Swami did as he was told. From that day onward, he rose early, bathed, and recited the Gayatri Mantra. The boy who once failed his examinations now did so well that his teacher suspected him of cheating.

"Oh, no!" said the boy; "but for the past few months I have been reciting the Gayatri Mantra every morning."

He continued to improve. He even won a one pound prize for poetry.

"I am proud of you," his father said. "I will match the school's prize with another whole pound."

Mahatma Anand Swami went on to publish a newspaper called *Milap* and became a millionaire who enjoyed all of life's successes.

The Gayatri Mantra can also saves lives. I can recall at least three motor bike accidents, from my own life.

In my first accident, as I drove slowly down an avenue in the nearby town of Billimora, a child darted from behind a parked carriage. It was too late to swerve, and I hurt the child badly. The people of the child's town were so cruel that they often beat drivers to death. Not long before, a truck driver had injured another child of that village and was found beaten to death at the scene of the accident. Certain that they would come after me, I recited the Gayatri Mantra with extra fervor. The child quickly recovered, and I remained safe.

Some years later, driving down a narrow road that ran through a small village, I saw, ahead of me, a group of women, huddled together, talking. I tapped my horn several times. The women looked up and scattered, herding their children with them. I waved in thanks and, as I passed them, began to accelerate. Suddenly, a child dashed across the road, looking for his mother. I slammed on the brake, as my motor bike ran over the child, trapping his leg between my brake pedal and the frame of the rear wheel. As I worked to free the child, I saw workers running towards me, brandishing weapons.

"Oh God, help me!" I prayed. Immediately the child's leg slipped out, unhurt, and I scooted away and reported the incident to the police.

One day, I was returning home on my motor bike from Surat, a city in the State of Gujarat, India. It was spring, and greenery blossomed everywhere. Preoccupied, admiring God's beauty, I headed too fast into a sharp curve. I skidded into an oncoming car, which knocked me 25 feet into the air. I closed my eyes, expecting to say my final Mantra. To my surprise, I landed with only a few bruises and a slightly swollen leg.

Gayatri Mantra benefits the physical person, but is even more powerful in purifying and strengthening the soul.

We shall document more instances of the power of this mantra in future publications.

Chapter 10

The New Age Force

Written by Shree Ram Sharma Acharya and translated and published by Brahmavarchas Research Institute.

It is an accepted fact that the New Age will evolve all by itself at the appropriate time. The Creator does not wish to see his beautiful, unparalleled creation destroyed, although it seems in a hurry to destroy itself. Man is its Master, carved by the Master-Creator using all his skills. Today there seems to be a race to completely destroy mankind. The demonic power of the intellect is trying to seize culture and destroy virtue and righteousness. However, that is an impossible task. The Godly Soul has assured us that whenever righteousness and virtue are in danger of extinction, he will appear in an incarnation to save it.

Lord Krishna says, in the Gita, "Whenever virtue declines and vice predominates, I incarnate. In visible form, I appear to destroy evil and re-establish virtue." Nature, which maintains a perfect balance in everything to keep itself going, has to maintain its cycle of movement, as it has been doing. The physical eye of the untaught man does not realize it, but one trained in the power of intuition can see that darkness is fast drifting away, yielding to a new dawn. As the old saying goes, "the old order yieldeth place the new."

The coming of the New Age has not aroused any controversy. It has been experienced in everyday life as a pre-ordained happening. Everyone knows who will win when all the creative forces join to challenge the destructive forces. Only Truth will ultimately prevail. Darkness reigns supreme until light takes over. When the call of work-consciousness, now heading towards dawn, driving destructive forces before it, is about to sound, feel assured that the enlightening smile of the New Age is on the horizon.

Whenever a new age dawns, it signifies the end of evil attitudes and the re-establishment of righteousness. It is like the removal of diseases by a different, but uncanny, therapy. Variety is the specialty of the New Age. In bygone days, the arrogance of evil threatened the world; to remove such evil, the Godly Soul took on earthly incarnations. It is not external wickedness that faces us this time, but mental corruption; only traditional intellect and wisdom can come to our rescue. Evil destroys itself in the face of Truth and, at this moment, the Divine Spiritual Intellect is descending upon Earth like the flow of the Ganges. We shall see God's incarnation in an era of spiritual consciousness. Irrational, evil forces have are so ingrained that they have almost reached the stage of faith; they cannot, therefore, be removed by the ordinary power of reason. The force necessary to deal with them must be much more powerful and on a higher spiritual level. It will take the form of Gayatri Age Force. The New Age Force is adequate to overcome any obscure evil. However, mental corruption is hidden. It buries itself quite deep in the form of personal ambition and faith and pursues evil aspirations. It is very difficult to meet this hidden challenge. One has to dive deep, find the enemy in its hideout and oust it, lock, stock and barrel. Only such a force as the Gayatri Force--the Prime Ordeal--is capable of accomplishing it. The evil born of ignorance cannot be removed unless the intellect, in the form of the lustrous Sun, manifests itself. Such a feat cannot be achieved by a mere courtly messenger. The Gayatri Force has to incarnate.

Any great accomplishment invokes the power of superior force. Even a small machine cannot function without adequate power. Similarly, the progress of an individual depends on the power one possesses. In order to effect a revolution, more than the expected force will have to be deployed.

When one studies past revolutions, one concludes that behind the revolution was a lot of force, in the form of support--aid, equipment, technique, effort--and thought--the main force. To make a successful revolution, tremendous social, economic, and political force must be employed from time to time. In the absence of such aid, equipment, and firm conviction, no revolution could succeed; so to re-establish good and destroy evil, one must harness a lot of aid and equipment to generate sufficient force. This time, the revolution is taking place on the spiritual field. Like the Kurukshetra, the battlefield where righteousness fought against unrighteousness, can be compared to the mental field.

One must assemble the necessary purifying equipment to prepare for such a battle. The aim of the

*tents pitched on this battlefield must be to purify the
intellect and wisdom of the people. Unless evil forces
and the evil thinking of people are reversed and
reoriented into constructive channels, no revolution is
possible. Only the Divine Force of the New Age, the
Gayatri Force, can bridle the fickle mind and
destructive tendencies of man and channel them in the
right direction. This is the mainspring which can
transform the present age into a New Age. Its goal is
to uproot all evil and establish creative actions. The
entire revolutionary process is divided into three parts:
psychological, technical, and social. These three parts
can be compared to the three currents of Gayatri. It
should be the aim of all people to purify themselves
against sins by the Gayatri Force.*

*Shapes of all men may look the same, but their
respective natures differ widely. A change in the heart
of a man soon changes his exterior. One can conceive
of the Gayatri Force as being instrumental in bringing
about such a change. For the coming of the New Age,
Gayatri will play the leading role.*

*One who looks at the Gayatri Mantra casually
may feel that it is an ordinary mantra, handed down
by Hindus as a useful aid in worship; its size and
ambit may very, very small. In reality, however,
Gayatri is very, very vast. The Gayatri Mantra is a
powerful force. It is embodied in the 24 letters that it
strings together. It can be described as a fountain of
life, as the backbone of Indian religion and culture.
The tuft is Gayatri; the sacred thread is Gayatri; the
most esteemed mantra is Gayatri. She is called the
mother of the Vedas, and the mother of the gods and
Goddesses. The splendor of Brahma originates in this*

mantra. *The history of India abounds in people who considered their motherland more sacred than even heaven and worked zealously to make it a heaven, nay the whole world. The mold in which such people were cast was the Gayatri mold, the pursuit of knowledge and penance for the benefit of everyone, performed by chanting the sacred Gayatri Mantra and pursuing Gayatri worship and meditation.*

The first ray of Gayatri fell on India. Naturally, therefore, its first and greatest impact should be noticed there. However one would not conclude that its sphere of influence is limited only to India; it extends to the entire world. The Japanese proudly claim that the Sun rises first in their country and call it "The Land of the Rising Sun". We can also say, without hurting their feelings, that the Sun does not shine only on Japan. "The Sun rises in the East, but, lo, the West is also bright." The Sun shines equally on all parts of the world and thus blesses everyone. One should understand Gayatri in the same universal sense. Her form can be conceived as that of the Mother of the entire Universe. The Mother form of all the Vedas put together is her first form. Yet even when thus described in the language of Sanskrit, employed in worship, she cannot be contained within that radius alone. Her field of activity and sphere of influence are far vaster. It is so vast indeed that the mantra can yield positive results for anyone and solve all problems, provided one approaches Gayatri with humility and faith. In the New Age to dawn, the role of Gayatri will be unparalleled, and so the Age is bound to be happier.

The power of kindling pure consciousness lies in the two-way force of Gayatri: knowledge and science.

Knowledge here means the higher, Divine knowledge, spiritual knowledge of the self which is gained by kindling the Divine intellectual knowledge. This knowledge is necessary for training one to elevate one's desire for highest spiritual attainments. Pursuit of higher knowledge, the knowledge of Self, and intellectual excellence is based on this. Aids like the pen, sound, vision, and hearing are all useful in the pursuit of this higher knowledge. Self-discipline, seeking the company of pious men, thinking and meditating on the Supreme Being as the symbol of Truth, Knowledge, and Eternal Bliss are the results of this knowledge.

Gayatri has another side, that of science. The different systems of worship and meditation are the main principles of this science. Broadly speaking, Gayatri worship seems like the worship of any other deity in order to realize one's goal, but this is not really so. In the hidden treasures of one's mind are many substantial abilities, replicas of Pure Consciousness, which can be re-kindled and harnessed for one's elevation. The failure to kindle the inner knowledge if the Self is poverty, and the effort to awaken it is prosperity. Those who successfully kindle the inner knowledge of the Self turn to it for their meditation and utilize it for a good cause are really great men. Such people will have historical achievements to their credit. Not only do they become blessed, but, because they are able to purify the atmosphere, they also bless those who come in contact with them.

Normally the body of a man is something over 5 feet in height and about 65 kg. in weight. This is not only so to the outward eye; its original force or power of consciousness is hidden in the eternal soul. Therefore, the soul assumes characteristics of the encasement in which it is placed. Like a chameleon, it can change the level of its color to suit the environment. The level of consciousness is responsible for its greatness or meanness. One cannot reach one's depth through the kindling of one's intellect. The purpose of the Gayatri is only worship and meditation. The only means of reaching the depth of one's conscious Self is found in the science of Gayatri. Man's important organs are three and the means to improve them and the power necessary to produce the desired fruits can be called true Gayatri worship and meditation. When one immerses oneself in this science, one gets the aid of many material things and benefits. In pursuit of the science of Gayatri, one's thinking and attitudes also get purified, and this is precisely the treatment advocated by the seers and sages of India.

God incarnates to annihilate the wicked and protect the righteousness by bringing about a proper balance and sense of value. The purpose of the incarnation is to correct whatever imbalance exists into proper balance. For this purpose, actions befitting the times are performed. These are called miracles. The purpose of all incarnations is one and the same: to remove all destructive forces and to re-establish Truth and righteousness. For this purpose alone the Supreme Godly Soul condescends to come down and incarnate.

Now what should be the nature of a given incarnation? It depends on the problems facing society at a given time. For this reason, although the Supreme

Soul is one and the same at all times, men see a difference in the nature and form of each incarnation.

The great Goddess Saraswati was born with her aids to help strengthen people's intellect for educating and energizing them. The Goddess Durga was born to combat evil and strengthen the community and thereby establish cooperation. Saraswati may be said to represent the conscience or the intellect preparing for a revolution in human society. Durga may be called the force for bringing about that revolution. Gayatri is the internal spiritual force for elevating mankind and the external force for imparting ethical sense. With the incarnation of Gayatri, the ethics of righteousness and spiritual science will open up fresh and revealing vistas. The science of ethics will also re-evolve as a result of the incarnation of Gayatri.

Whenever the purpose and propriety of any incarnation is discussed, it is the practice to give credit to the incarnate leader. This is the visualization through the physical eye only. Practically, the changes that revolutionize any age are the accumulated results occurring in the subtle world due to terrific forces of consciousness that generate in the spiritual firmament. Innumerable conscious souls, influenced by such forces, act together and discharge their assigned duties. This is the principle behind every incarnation. A camera undoubtedly catches the image of a man's face more clearly. Even so, every part of him is important. Thus the credit goes to the leader- the Incarnate. In principle, an incarnation is the revolutionary spirit of that age working in the subtle (astral) world.

The Gayatri New Age Force incarnated first in the traditional way, through Brahma, as the Mother. Then the Mother's seven incarnations were expressed in the form of utterances which became known to the world through the seven famous Rushis. The ninth incarnation was in the form of Vishwamitra. We find that the presiding deity of the Gayatri meter is the Sun, its seer being Vishwamitra. Through the medium of Brahma was born the Mother, through the medium of the seven Rushis was born the Godly Mother, and through Vishwamitra was the Mother of the Universe incarnated. The tenth incarnation to be is that of Gayatri, which heralds the beginning of the New and beginning of the New and prosperous Age, an Age which the intelligent can see with their inner eye.

The deformities of our age run deeper than one can imagine. Purifying one's thoughts and consciousness, and meticulously removing the danger posed by the over-zealous pursuit of passions, is the only panacea for the many ills plaguing the world today. It is the focal point of all the hopes for a bright future, and the forces of remedy and upliftment revolve around it. The New Age can become an age of revolution by ousting the forces of evil and inactivity and sowing the seeds of good and righteous actions. By the same token, it can also be regarded as the age of incarnation of the consciousness of the highest order.

Chapter 11

Yagna

In Indian culture, Gayatri is the mother of all knowledge and YAGNA is the fuel that powers the Vedic religion. Gayatri guides the practitioner towards good thoughts and Yagna symbolizes the practitioner's good deeds. Together, good thoughts and good deeds clear the path to universal peace and human welfare.

The little time and money that you invest in a Yagna ceremony yield rich benefits, just as a few grains of well-planted wheat yield a golden harvest. Offering material items at a Yagna sows seeds in heavenly fields: And as the power of heaven is a thousand times greater than that of earth, so performing the Yagna ceremony yields infinitely greater rewards than cultivating the soil.

The Yagna ceremony aids powerful elements ever-present in the atmosphere, killing thousands of disease-carrying, air-borne bacilli. Modern medicines may help those who take them, but the purifying smoke of Yagna protects all life--humans, animals, birds, beasts, insects, and vegetation.

Our mechanized "civilization" poisons the atmosphere until mankind grows physically and mentally weaker. The Yagna can be our remedy; Yagna shields us against diseases. The scientific benefits of Yagna have been accepted by leading scientists throughout the world.

"By burning any medicine," says Dr. Hyhneman, the founder of the science of Homeopathy, *"a very small part of the smoke[,] which we call fragrance[,] spreads into the surrounding atmosphere and, when inhaled, goes into the lungs and brings new light ... "*

"Mixing ghee [a derivative of butter] and sugar," continues Dr. Haffkine, *"and burning them creates smoke which kills the germs of certain diseases and stimulates a secretion from certain glands related to the wind-pipe, which fills our heart and mind with pleasure."*

"Burning sugar and its smoke," adds the French scientist Prof. Tilward, *"can help purify the atmosphere. It kills the germs of T.B., measles, small pox, and cow pox."*

"After [many] successful experiments," says the Russian scientist Shirowich, *"we have collected the following data about the cow and Yagna, [much of] which even people of India do not know:*

1. *Cow's milk contains [elements that] protect [us] from atomic radiation;*

2. *[Therefore,] houses with cowdung-covered floors enjoy . . . protection from atomic radiation; and*

3. *If cow's ghee is put into fire, its smoke will greatly reduce the [harmful] effects of atomic radiation.*

"This process is known as 'Yagna' in Indian languages."

We can appreciate the value of protecting the universe from the poisonous effects of pollution and radioactivity. Yagna provides a way to pray to God while protecting all life.

Yagna symbolizes the mystic ideal of giving away all your possessions. As such, it represents a form of spiritual socialism. In Yagna, the practitioner symbolically gives to all humankind by offering favorite things, such as ghee, sweets, fruits, and medicinal herbs, to the fire of Yagna. This teaches us to make the best use of our power and prowess, knowledge of wealth, status and influence--to apply them, not only to ourselves, but to society at large.

Nature, herself, exhibits the ideal of Yagna. The waters of the ocean evaporate into clouds; the winds blow them around the globe and give them back on Earth as life-giving rain. Trees and other vegetation live for others, providing flower and fruit that life may flourish. The sun, the moon and the winds exist, not for their own benefit, but for the well-being of all living organisms. Wherever we cast eyes, the world of nature proclaims the ideal of Yagna. With little labor and expense, the performer of Yagna serves the entire universe.

Chapter 12

Third Pilgrimage to the Himalayas - Sowing of the Seeds of Rushi Traditions

Written by Shree Ram Sharma Acharya and translated by Shree Satyanarayan Pandya.

After the work at Mathura had been set up on a satisfactory footing, I received the third call from the Himalayas in which there was indication about the next steps which were to be taken. There had been this time considerable pressure of work which had resulted in fatigue although success was achieved. Under these circumstances, this invitation for "charging the battery" was most encouraging.

I set out for the journey on the prescribed day. There was no difficulty as I was familiar with the route, the cold was also not so bitter as it was at the time of my first journey. I did not feel loneliness also. I was escorted by Gurudev's messenger from Gomukh to Nandanvan. The anxious auspicious moment for which I was keen throughout the journey ultimately arrived. After exchange of adorations and blessings, the chain of guidance started.

Gurudev said, "You have to leave Mathura and come to stay at Hardwar and start the work of rejuvenating Rushi traditions. You will recall that when you came here for the first time you had met Rushis living in this region in astral body and each of them had expressed disappointment on the disappearance of their traditions and you had given words that you will accomplish this work. This time you have been summoned for this purpose.

"God has no physical form. Whenever something important is sought to be achieved, Rushis, who remain engrossed in Penance impart their power to Godly souls, great persons and get the work done through them. Rushi Vishvamitra took Lord Ram 7th Incarnation to his hermitage on the pretext of defending his yagna, trained him in Gayatri and Savitri (scientific knowledge), and got the castle of devilishness tumbled down and the kingdom of truth and righteousness established. Shri Lord Krishna 8th Incarnation had gone to Sandipan Rushi and returned after he had been duly trained in Geeta, Mahabharat and the method of working of Sudama Rushi. Ancient scriptures are full of description that Rushis created great men and got important work accomplished through them, although they themselves always remained engrossed in Penance, yoga, research, etc. It is this work which you have to accomplish.

"The seer of Gayatri mantra was Rushi Vishvamitra who had lived in Sapt Sarovar, Hardwar and had acquired proficiency in Gayatri. That place is now reserved for you. You will be able to find it out easily. Name it as Shanti-kunj, Gayatri-teerth and sow the seeds of all the works which used to be performed by the Rushis when they used to live in their physical form in the ancient past. Now they are all in astral

form. They need a physical medium to get their work done. I, too, had felt a similar need, found in you a competent person, contacted and engaged you in this program. These Rushis have also the same aspiration. You have to newly sow the seeds of old Rushi traditions, which is no doubt a difficult task but you will be getting patronage, blessings and grants from me as well as all those Rushis and you will proceed undeterred."

Briefly describing the incomplete work of the Rushis, I was told to acquaint people with the power of Gayatri supreme-mantra according to the tradition of Vishvamitra Rushi and to establish an endowed place with extrasensory spiritual power, called Gayatri-teerth; to write books and eighteen volumes of Pragya Puran in Vyas tradition; to extend the science and philosophy of Yog-accomplishing in Rushi Patanjali tradition; to build up refined atmosphere by eradicating immorality from the minds of the people according to Rushi Parasuram tradition; to conduct scientific research and revive popular use of medicinal herbs according to Rushi Charak tradition; to pacify and set right mental disorders by wholesome treatment of science and philosophy of yagna in Rushi Yagyavalkya tradition; to establish a hermitage for promoting the growth of good habits and character-building in Rushi Jamadagni tradition; to lead wandering life of a religious mendicant (parivrajak) to impart true knowledge and advice for the extention of religious consciousness in Godly Rushi Narad tradition; to provide guidance through the medium of religion to the administrative set-up in the tradition of Rushi Aryabhatta; to build up high intellectual spiritual centers at different places in Saint Shankaracharya tradition; to promote all-round health with the help of proper dieting according to Rushi Pippalad tradition and to convene high intellectual spiritual organized planning from place to place for educating the masses according to Rushi Soot-Shounik tradition. Gurudev also indicated the outline of establishing Brahmavarchas Research Institute for conducting research in scientific method on the lines of Kanad Rushi according to the scientific traditions of science of material things (Atharv-Veda).

It was explained in detail what I have to do at Hardwar and how difficulties coming in my way are to be resolved. I assimilated each and every word uttered by Gurudev. The last time when I visited the Himalayas, I was to act according to the directions given by Gurudev alone. This time I was loaded with the additional burden of huge tasks. This poor donkey was to be more cautious and more laborious. Without elaborating, Gurudev simply gave a hint that after doing all this, I will have to pay a fourth visit to the Himalayas and shoulder still higher responsibilities and take measures to adopt the astral body.

I was informed that the method of working at Hardwar would be more difficult than that at Mathura, the aggression of devilish elements will have to be faced, and there will be several ups and downs. In view of difficult times, I was directed to stay in the Himalayas only for six months and not a year. After explaining where and how I had to live and perform my daily routine, I was told that I should regard it as a joint program of Gurudev and all the Rushis. I assured Gurudev that for me he was a representative of the Supreme God, all the Rushis and Gods and all his directions will be complied with so long as I was alive.

Our talks ended. After bidding farewell, Gurudev disappeared. I was escorted up to Gomukh by his assistant. It is hardly necessary to mention the places where I was required to stay as they are inaccessible places in the Himalayas.

While returning, I stayed at the place indicated by Gurudev in Hardwar. It was the place where seven Rushi penanced. It was lying deserted and was for sale. It ejected water. The Ganges used to flow through this land in the past. The site was quite pleasing. The owner of the land was contacted, a bargain was made, and the deal was reduced into writing. The advice of the advisers was of little use because they did not know the manner and the purpose for which buildings were sought to be built on this land. I had to decide and do this work myself. Ultimately, Shanti-kunj, Gayatri teerth, was built and established.

Chapter 13

Miracle

Shree Ram Sharma does not like his devotees to talk about his miracles. Maganbhai P. Gandhi used to talk a lot about Shree Ram Sharma's miracles. Shree Ram wrote a letter to Maganbhai, asking him to talk, not about his miracles, but about his work. Shree Ram says that performing miracles comes naturally from knowing God, because what appear to be miracles are all in tune with God's law. "Miracles" are not important.

The most important spiritual accomplishments are a saint's work and conquering delusion. Through righteous battle and correct behavior, saints attain their goal.

Shree Ram believes that all human beings have the same power. The only apparent difference in most people is that they do not recognize and develop their hidden "super"-natural power.

Shree Ram has performed many miracles. Space permits discussion of only a few.

In the year 1969, while on a business trip, I chanced to meet my cousin, Shri Mohanbhai, on a train, while travelling through the Indian city of Surat, in Gujarat State. We talked until we had caught up on family matters, and then lapsed into silence.

Eventually, he pulled out a Gita, a religious book, and began to read.

"Do you have anything in there," I nodded towards his briefcase, "that I could read?"

"Just the thing," he smiled. He reached back into his case and handed me a book about prophecy. It contained many predictions by well-known Indian mystics that an angel would be born. The editor sought to establish that Shree Ram Sharma Acharya is an angel of God. I wanted to discover for myself whether this man could fulfill the prophecies.

I decided that I had to see this Shree Ram Sharma Acharya for myself.

As chance--or was it more than chance?-- would have it, I learned that Shree Ram was coming to Baroda, about 125 miles away, the very next day.

My cousin, Shree Mohanlal, and I rose early and reached Baroda by 5:00 a.m. After some inquiries as to what path Shree Ram might take through the auditorium, I took a seat as close as possible to the stage. My cousin took the same seat in the next row. We wanted to be able to see his feet as he passed.

A silence swept through the hall as Shree Ram entered. As He passed my seat, I craned my neck; I could see my cousin doing the same.

"Did you notice something?" I asked him.

"What did you see?" he asked me.

"His toe nails are as red as nail polish," I answered.

"I noticed the same thing," my cousin said.

We looked up to where Shree Ram now sat on stage, discussing the Gayatri Mantra and the Vedic religion. Between his two eyebrows, in the middle of his forehead, we saw the symbol for the second day moon, as clear and as natural as the moon itself in the sky.

I decided to take the Mantra Diksha (Initiation Program) from Shree Ram that day.

Those who were not already wearing the Yagnopavit--the sacred thread that dangles around the neck and down to the hips of those formally initiated into the Hindu religion--were asked to move to the front row. I followed after all the small children.

Before I begin your initiation, Shree Ram had said, I should like a bargain from each of you--to give up one of your bad habits or one habit that you enjoy.

With that, Shree Ram began the ceremony.

As the ceremony progressed, I grew more and more distraught. I loved eating meat. And I enjoyed alcohol. At that time I used to drink an entire "fifth" every day. I should have to sacrifice these things, I thought, to keep my bargain, for these are the things which I love most.

I began praying from my heart, mentally, to Shree Ram, to give me the courage and strength to fulfill my part of the bargain. I repeated my prayer from the depths of my heart.

Suddenly, Shree Ram asked his disciple to stop the ceremony.

"Whoever is worried about sacrificing the eating of meat and the drinking of alcohol should not worry," he said. "I shall take care of your craving, and of you. Concentrate on your initiation."

As soon as he spoke, my worries melted. I felt sure that he had read my mind and understood my thoughts. I remember feeling filled with joy that he would give me some of his strength to fulfill my promised sacrifices.

At the end of the Mantra-Diksha ceremony, each initiate bowed his or her head and took Shree Ram's blessing, in turn. Shree Ram moved down the aisle, touching each initiate lightly on the back, between the shoulder blades.

When I went to him, I bowed my head expectantly. To my surprise, he simply placed the third and fourth fingers of his right hand on my left cheek, and, from that moment on, my desire for meat and alcohol vanished. I thanked him from the bottom of my heart.

My cousin also waited in line; but his thoughts were different. "If you are truly the incarnation, the son of God," he thought, "then when I bow before you and touch your feet for your blessing, you will give me a hard thrashing, with your hand, on my back. If you do that, then I will know that the prophecy is true and that you are here to fulfill it."

Shree Mohanlal watched as my turn came. His brow wrinkled as Shree Ram touched my cheek. The line moved, and he stood before Shree Ram. My cousin bent to touch Shree Ram's feet, and "Guruji" thrashed him hard on the back. They both laughed.

Some months later, Guruji visited Bombay. I went to see him again. So many people waited for his blessing. He called me first.

He asked how I was. He also asked how my family and my business were.

"Everything is fine," I replied. As I answered, however, strange thoughts coursed through my mind, yet I could not bring myself to state them, and so I asked him to help me keep my consciousness focused on God. "And I will work for you," I said.

"Speak your thoughts!" my inner mind shouted, but I could not.

Shree Ram finished passing his blessing to all who waited. Then, as if reading my mind, he called me back to him.

"You may ask whatever you want," he said.

However, I could not. "Just keep my thoughts fixed in God," I stammered. "And I shall work for you."

Years later, as my spiritual development increased, I understood why those particular requests, if asked and granted, would have restricted my growth and welfare.

From 1970 to 1984 my life seemed sprinkled with miracles. Then, in 1984, I wanted to return to India to look after my old parents.

I wrote to Shree Ram, asking his permission. Since Shree Ram was busy working to transform his physical body into his five astral bodies, his wife, Mataji, who was managing his organization, replied. She said that I should not go.

Determined, I went anyway. I should have listened: my trip did not help my parents as I had hoped, and I returned to America with nothing to show for my troubles and thousands of dollars poorer.

In the year 1987, I found myself constantly worried without reason. I knew that my worrying was useless, but could not clear my mind. My tension increased. I never mentioned these concerns to Guruji. Nevertheless, in one of Mataji's letters to me, she wrote,

"Keep your mind free from worry. Try to be happy. My blessing is with you."

As I read her words, my tension vanished. From thousands of miles away, Shree Ram and Mataji take care of Shree Ram's disciples.

Shree Ram's talk is sweet and lovable. He welcomes everybody, treats all with respect, and no one who has taken his problems to him has returned home dissatisfied.

A friend of mine, poor, unemployed, with a wife and four children, wrote several letters to Shree Ram, but never received a reply.

"Why don't you go in person," I advised.

"Without money," my friend replied, "how could I go?"

So I lent him the Rs.200/- for the journey, and he went to see "Guruji".

Shree Ram welcomed him.

At the proper time, my friend bowed.

Shree Ram gave his blessing, and then asked, "How can I help you?"

My friend related his misfortune and asked for Guruji's help.

"How can I help you?" Shree Ram answered. "You have done so many sins in your previous life, that you must suffer for them now. However, as you have come to see me, I give my blessing to you. I assure you that you will get a job."

My friend returned home and, within a week, had a new job.

In 1971, Dada Gurudev called Shree Ram back to the Himalayas. Most of his disciples feared that he might never return.

So my wife and children and I went for a blessing.

One of his disciples in England, however, could not come, and wrote to say so.

You do not need to come to me, Guruji replied, but whenever you want to see me just pray for me and I shall be there for you.

The disciple returned home from work the evening that Shree Ram's letter arrived and read it carefully. He sat down for his prayers and remembered Shree Ram in them. In less than five minutes, he saw Shree Ram, physically, before him. He bowed down, took Shree Ram's blessings, and enjoyed the pleasure of a long, personal talk.

Guruji has used his Divine Power five documented times to restore those whom physicians have pronounced dead back to life.

Mr. Maganlal P. Ghandi, of Navsari, Gujarat, India, was one of five people to die during the Gayatri Yagna ceremony at Anand. Guruji saw his body and intoned, "Arise". Instantly, the dead man got up.

Vijaykumar Sharma, of Patna, Bihar State, died on December 17, 1969; Guruji brought him back to life.

The son of L.N. Tripathi, Class I Officer at the Bhilai steel plant, fell from a garden swing and died of a brain injury. Shree Ram restored the boy's life.

On April 10, 1981, Gorakhnath Srivastav, of Patna, died of a heart attack at 11:00 p.m., after performing the Gayatri Anusthan for six of the nine prescribed days. Shree Ram was informed, and returned him to life.

A girl from the State of Gujarat came to study at Guruji's camp at Shanti Kunj. A year after her course ended, she died, and Guruji restored her life.

Maganlal P. Ghandi of Navsari lived for ten years after Shree Ram restored him. Some time after his funeral, his widow came and cried before Shree Ram. Shree Ram consoled her.

"But now he has truly died," she wailed.

I know, answered Shree Ram, for I attended his funeral. It was I, dressed as one of the mourners, who put holy water of the River Ganges in his mouth as he died.

Guruji smiled. Your husband has already been reborn, he told her. The mother recently brought him to your house. You fondled him and gave the baby Rs.5/- .

Shri Maganlal's widow returned home in peace.

For seven years a man felt almost unbearable pain in his stomach and often passed blood in his urine. His doctor operated, but in vain. The man decided to visit Badrinath and Kedarnath, sacred places in the Himalayas. On the way, he paused to rest at Delhi.

The pain started up again, so unbearable that he cancelled his journey. He would return home after meeting with Shree Ram at Shanti Kunj.

You are on a pilgrimage, Guruji told him, to Badrinath and Kedarnath. Continue, without worry. For medicine, take, from Mataji, some of the ashes of our Yagna.

The man did so, completed his journey, and returned home cured.

Another man, soon after the death of his father, took his family to Shanti Kunj to see Shree Ram. If Guruji asks, he told his child, tell him that you would like to see Grandfather.

The man sent his son to Guruji.

"What can I do for you." Guruji asked, as usual.

"I wish to see my dead grandfather," the boy replied.

Come with me, Shree Ram said.

Guruji took the boy into the Meditation Room.

"Who is standing there?" he asked.

"Grandfather!" the boy cried, for he saw the old man as clearly as though he were still alive. The boy ran off to tell his parents, who, although sorry that they had missed Grandfather, understood that Guruji had recalled him for the person who needed to see him the most.

When Indian invaded East Pakistan (Bangladesh), the American Navy steamed to the latter's aid. Shree Ram Sharma delayed them. Seven disciples dreamed, that night, that two giant hands rose up from the sea, before the advancing fleet. One hand grabbed a flying helicopter and crushed it like a giant insect.

Only a few sailors, and perhaps the Pentagon, know for sure what happened that day, but the fleet proceeded no further, and waited off-shore.

In 1984 a teacher named Budhabhai, who lived in the town of Chhipadi in the State of Gujarat, resolved to build a new Cultural and Spiritual Development Center for Shree Ram's disciples. To raise money, he had to pledge his own jewelry.

With only eight days until the ribbon-cutting
ceremony, he rented a cement mixer to speed up
construction and meet the deadline. When it came
time to return the machine, he had no way of knowing
that two young children had hidden themselves inside.

As the teacher and some friends drove the
machine down the road, it struck a low-hanging
branch. The jolt flipped the nozzle of the mixer and
tossed the two children smack under the wheels.

Neighbors ran to help.

Together they lifted the machine and pulled the
boys out. One suffered only some small cuts--he was
lucky. Budhabhai's son was not; his head was
crushed.

Carefully, they rushed him to the Civil Hospital
in Ahmedabad, the nearest large city. The latest
equipment and best doctors were pressed into service,
but to no avail.

"I am sorry," one of the surgeons told Budhabhai
and his wife. "His brain has hemorrhaged. There is
nothing that we can do here to save the boy. Take him
home, make him comfortable, and pray to God. Only
God can save him."

Shree Ram had come to Chhipadi that morning to
attend the opening ceremony. After the ceremony,
Shree Ram went on to his next scheduled stop, at
Ahmedabad. There devotees told him about the
accident.

As soon as Shree Ram heard the story of
Budabhai's son, he rushed to the hospital.

He placed his hand on the child's head and
blessed him. The P.R.O. (head) of the hospital looked
on doubtfully.

SHANTI KUNJ - QUARTERS FOR STUDENTS

However, the boy began to improve. Day by day, he got stronger, more cheerful.

"Who was that Saint?" Mr. Rameshbhai Joshi, the P.R.O., asked, "For he surely saved the boy's life."

The child has since fully recovered, and he now gets better grades than he ever did before.

Not long ago, a leak in a Union Carbide factory in Bophal, India, killed over 2,000 townspeople in one gruesome afternoon. Without discrimination, the poison killed young and old, killed mother and child. Yet, miraculously, every single member of Shree Ram's local Gayatri Pariwar survived unscathed. In fact, many members of the Gayatri Pariwar volunteered to aid the suffering. Others drove as near the site as officials permitted and performed the Yagna ceremony from the back of a tractor trailer, so that the purifying fumes of the Yagna fire could cleanse the air of Bophal.

Shree Ram Sharma has re-joined a young boy's broken leg that had been amputated to save the boy's life by the family's doctor. He has, without surgery, removed a tumor from the stomach of a woman disciple. His blessing enabled many an infertile woman to conceive.

Shree Ram has down unaccountable miracles. Many more will be told in a future book called *Miracles of the Messiah*.

AN IDOL OF SHREE GODDESS GAYATRI AND CONTINUOUS LAMP

Chapter 14

Shree Ram & Shanti Kunj

To make and carry out a five-year plan for a nation is like moving heaven and earth. From his retreat, or Ashram, at Shanti Kunj, in Hardwar, Northern India, where Rushi Vishwamitra and seven Rushis once did penance, Shree Ram intends to move earth closer to heaven.

This Ahsram in the Himalayan Mountains represents Devatma, the Divine soul.

The Ashram has living facilities for 240 devotees, a large lecture and meeting hall, and symbolic temples for Ganga, the goddess of the River Ganges, and Uttarakhand, a scale model of the full Himalayan Mountain Range, complete with statues of many prominent Rushis who live there. A Temple of the Goddess Gayatri dominates the Ashram.

Shree Ram's Residence has three floors. The ground floor houses the Ashram's administrative offices. Mataji Bhagwsati Devi uses most of the second floor to manage Shree Ram's international organization. A special room houses the icon of Shree Goddess Gayatra Mata (mother) and the Akhand-deep, a special Ghee-burning lamp that has burned continuously since 1926, when Shree Ram was fifteen. Shree Ram, himself, stays on the third floor, which has one bedroom, one meeting room, and a meditation room.

To awaken the dormant power of the land upon which the Ashram sits, 27 maidens personally trained by Mataji performed 24 puruscharans, or recitations, of 2.4 million mantras. Then Mataji trained more than 100 young women in the arts of music and public speaking and sent them throughout the country in groups of five to deliver religious discourses. Their performance was instrumental in awakening women from blind adherence to tradition and dogma.

The permanent residents of Shanti Kunj, devotees who come for training, and visitors join together to recite a purushcharan of 2.4 million Gayatri mantras daily.

Shree Ram resurrected the science of Gayatri and the Vedic institution of Yagna (sacrifice). Gayatri--combining the powers of Creation, Sustenance, and Destruction--guides the destiny of the world. The science of Gayatri, therefore, encompasses a complete philosophy of life, from birth to death. The Gayatri force can bring peace to a strife-torn world. Its ancient, universal force can propel us into the Age of Harmony. Guruji combines Gayatri with the sacrificial spirit of Yagna to reverse the aggressive self-centeredness that has plagued much of the Twentieth Century.

Education lays the groundwork for the ethical, moral, and intellectual revolution that will convert men into Godly souls and establish Heaven on Earth.

At the Ashram's Brahmavarchas Research Center, religious-minded graduates and post-graduates in many fields, particularly medicine and Ayurved (herbal medicine), volunteer their time to integrate the findings of science with the insights of religion. They have, for example, accumulated evidence that adopting spiritual principles in one's everyday life effects changes in the body's physiology as well as in its mental processes.

In the phyto-chemistry and gas analysis wing, scientific research into the biochemical and immunological changes in material bodies following the Yagna ceremony have yielded particularly interesting results, showing a favorable influence of the Yagna ceremony on both physical and mental diseases, on animal and vegetable growth, and in refining the atmosphere above and the environment about us.

Simultaneously, physicians using spirometers and cardiac monitors have documented that penance, meditation, and yoga increase the reserve capacity of both the lungs and heart.

The sound laboratory uses oscilloscopes to display the sound patterns of the Vedic mantras. Sophisticated tests of meaningful versus incoherent mantras compare corresponding changes in the subject's blood chemistry and other body parameters.

The psychometry lab begins with a battery of psychological tests to establish each subject's "learning profile." Subjects then begin both their studies and an individually/randomly assigned regiment of meditation and yoga. Finally, technicians measure each subject's academic progress against his or her predicted profile.

Soon, the Ashram hopes to open its endocrinology laboratory to measure hormonal changes induced by both modern medicines and traditional medicinal plants. Currently, a large herb garden, fostering over 300 varieties of rare and common plants, supports the "Barefoot Doctor" Program.

The School of Languages at Shanti Kunj prepares students to carry Shree Ram's message to all nations. The School has established departmental studies in the dialects of Gujarat, Rajasthan, Madhya pradesh, Uttar pradesh, Bihar, Himachal Haryana, Orrisa, and Maharashtra. Its dean hopes to cover at least all of India in the next few years.

Within two short years, Shree Ram's devotees erected 2400 teaching centers around India to spread the message of Yug Chetna, the awakening to the new light. More than 12,000 book carts, pushed by devotees of Shree Ram, carry his books throughout his own city and to nearby towns and outlying areas. The Ashram also operates its own small printing press.

Thus has Shree Ram become a touchstone, who turns the base around him to gold.

Many Government officials, impressed by the organization at Shanti Kunj, have sent personnel there for moral and cultural development. Several schools and universities have accepted the works of Shree Ram as textbooks.

Newcomers to the Ashram first receive examinations for their physical and spiritual health and a prescription for spiritual improvement. Millions more visit Shanti Kunj to have the Yagnapavit ("sacred thread" of Hindu initiation) ceremony performed for themselves or their children.

In India, as in many Third World nations, the burden of providing dowries for unmarried daughters can strangle even the wealthiest of families. However, at both Shanti Kunj and Tapobhumi, Shree Ram's center in Mathura, couples marry inexpensively.

At Shanti Kunj, volunteers in many professions labor day and night to bring about the Sat Yug. For example, highly qualified physicians volunteer their time so that the needy can receive, with dignity, the best health care available. The strength of Shanti Kunj's volunteer corps swells daily. Such dedication to the work of God will propel the world into the New Era.

In his almost 80 years, Shree Ram has performed many astonishingly difficult tasks. Some have said that most men would need 800 years to do as much for mankind. Shree Ram does it by making the most of each moment of his life. He has written enough articles to fill all of his publications until the year 2000 A.D. For example, he initiated a program at Shanti Kunj to write an 18-volume encyclopedia called Pragna Puran, of which eight volumes have already been published. He decided to set down one of his ideas in a new, eight-page manuscript every day.

To date, over 500 manuscripts have been written, translated into the various languages of India, and disseminated.

Shree Ram does not simply write books that tell others how to live happy and prosperous lives; he applies his principles to his own life. For instance, Shree Ram once visited Africa and stayed in the house of this friend and disciple, Shree Tuljashankar Dave. Common practice dictates that the host provide a wide variety of tasty foods to an honored guest, and Shree Tuljashankar Dave outdid himself. After dinner on the first night, Guruji took his host aside and asked him to prepare only one vegetable and chopati the next day.

Indeed, Shree Tuljashankar Dave prepared lunch as his guest requested.

"At least, have one more chopati," the host urged. "They are warm and easily digested."

Guruji replied that one should take just enough food to maintain good bodily fitness, for eating in excess of the body's needs invites sickness in oneself and means keeping others hungry.

When Guruji returned to Shanti Kunj from this visit, he distributed the gifts he had received among the children and volunteers.

Guruji has no enmity for those who would sabotage his program for human progress. On January 8, 1984, Shree Ram sat alone in his room when a hired killer burst in. He pointed a revolver at Shree Ram and pulled the trigger five times, yet not one bullet left the barrel. Panicked, the assassin dropped the revolver and lunged forward with a slaughtering knife. Although he slashed repeatedly, the blade did not penetrate Guruji's body, but left only 12 surface cuts.

During the attack, Guruji refused to call out for help but, rather, showed the man how to escape, lest his enraged disciples tear the man to pieces.

As the man fled, Guruji called for a doctor.

"You've lost a lot of blood," the doctor said. "We should consider a transfusion."

No, Guruji answered, for I have not put either salt or sugar in my body since I was 15. I will not risk taking either from strange blood.

"Hmmm", said the doctor. "In that case, you'd better increase your diet--drink lots of fluids and eat foods rich in the nutrients you've lost."

Again Guruji refused.

When we cannot afford enough milk for all our children, he said, we shall not divert additional food to me.

Meanwhile, word of the attack spread, and a crowd gathered outside.

"Let's find the murderer!" they shouted.

No, Guruji said. It is not for us to take revenge. Justice will punish him in her own time.

Indeed, some years later the would-be killer was wounded when a bomb he planted blew up on him. Under police interrogation he admitted many past crimes, including the attack on Shree Ram. Both he and the person who ordered the attack received death sentences from the courts.

During the early 1970's, Shree Ram commissioned a group of American scientists to try and discover why many of his "miracles" worked. If the physical reasons could be found, Guruji reasoned perhaps he could teach all people to tap into the tremendous powers of the body. Under scientific observation, for example, Shree Ram drank a vial of the deadly poison potassium cyanide without apparent ill effects. Although the phenomena have been recorded, as of this writing the scientific basis for Shree Ram's miracles unfortunately continue to elude observers.

En route home to India, Shree Ram stopped in Rome for a meeting with Pope Paul I. The Pope, who does not bow to any man, who bows only to God or Jesus, bowed to Shree Ram Sharma for a blessing. Why? Did His Holiness recognize Shree Ram's Divine power? Did he he see in Shree Ram the promise, even the person, of the Reincarnation?

At this age, Shree Ram's physical body looks frail, but a tremendous life-force emanates from him. As recently as a a few years ago, he was able to turn aside the charge of a mad bull.

Shree Ram Sharma Acharya has warned that the 12 years from 1989 to 2000 A.D. will be years of transition and will see an inordinate amount of pain, trouble, and suffering. Such a period is known as a Treaty-Age. Jesus said, *"For then there will be a great tribulation such as has not been from the beginning of the world until now nor will be"* (Matthew 24:21).

"But immediately after the tribulation of those days, the sun will be darkened, and the moon will not give her light, and the stars will fall from heaven and the power of heaven will be shaken" (Mark 13:24-25).

I believe that these are the times foretold in Revelations-the time of trumpets, bowls and seals.

Shree Ram has sounded the warning.

Yet, God sent Jonah to Nineveh to warn its citizens that in forty days would the city be destroyed. So the people of Nineveh fasted and prayed and God relented and the city was saved. So Shree Ram has requested, and started, a massive, collective appeal to heaven known as the Era of the Treaty of Mahapuruscharan. In Sanskrit, a Treaty of Mahapuruscharan is a definite commitment to perform a specified number of Gayatri Mantras within a specific period of time to appease God, to turn aside his anger, and thereby to replace the prophesied calamities with sanctified harmony. The correct number mantras must be performed exactly as prescribed, at the specified time, for the proper length of time.

The Era of the Treaty of Mahapuruscharan can begin any Sunday. It can be launched by ordinary men, women, boys, girls, of any age, an caste, any religion, any creed willing to invest less time than it takes to eat breakfast.

Whoever would like to help launch the Mahapuruscharan should recite the Gayatri Mantra, while facing east, for a minimum of fifteen minutes, early every Sunday morning. After reciting pray for peace from your own heart or using the following prayer:

> Oam! Dyough Shantih
> Aantariksha gunh Shantih
> Prithivih Shantih
> Aapah Shantih
> Aoshdhayah Shantih
> Vanaspatayah Shantih
> Vishve devah Shantih
> Brahma Shantih
> Sarva gunh Shantih
> Shantih reva Shantih
> Sa ma Shanti redhi.

May the heavens, the sky and the earth be serene! May the waters, the herbs, the plants, the universal gods, the supreme god and the entire creation be peaceful! May peace herself bestow inner contentment upon me!

> Oam! Vishwani deva Savitar,
> Duritani parasuva,
> Yad bhadram,

Tanna aa sura.

Hail to thee! The all inspiring sun! Drive away all our sins! Bring us all that is blessed.

Oam! Shantih Shantih Shantih
Sarvarishta Sushantir bhavatu,

Let peace prevail. Let all the three types of miseries be alleviated.

Those who worship a formless God might picture a source of Divine Light, the golden color of the sun. Envision the bright, golden rays entering your body and lighting it with Divine power. After the recitation, carry a vessel of water outside and lift your arms to the sun. As you pour the water slowly to the earth, close your eyes and picture rain failing to the land, to form a vapro that rises up into the clouds, which in turn rains back on Earth and waters all flowers, fruits and vegetables. Envision the entire world as a single, beautiful garden where people live happily and peacefully.

If you wish, fast on Sundays, although it is not compulsory. Millions of devotees of Shree Ram recite the gayatri spell to hasten the change from this era into the Age of Harmony. Each devotee dedicates 108 recitations every day to this mission.

Millions of devotees of Shree Ram recite daily 108 repetitions of the Gayatri Spell to hasten the transition from this era to the Sat Yug, the Age of Harmony.

Shree Ram Sharma Acharya has given birth to a creative upheaval. He shows us, in his book *My Will and Heritage*, that "*the willpower of even ordinary people is effective. As public opinion, it exerts pressure before which even those in power must yield. The*

Pragya Abhiyan [Shree Ram's movement; the words mean 'Kindling of High Intellectual True Knowledge'], will awaken public opinion. Under its scrutiny, people will want to employ their energy and skill for constructive, rather than destructive, ends. The power of minds joined together makes for a great force. It produces miracles in whichever direction it proceeds.

"The problems of the present day are interwoven, whether they appear to stem from pollution, the arms build-up, immorality and licentiousness, or 'Acts of God', like epidemics and famine. It is not possible to solve one by itself for they are all intertwined. Solutions are, therefore, bound to proliferate if we resolve to pursue them.[2]

"Two main powers make or mar harmony:. One is the power of arms and money, and the other is the power of intellect or organization. People have, in the past, been subdued and corrupted by the power of arms and money and compelled to act against their wishes. This is demonic power. In the future, Divine power must be called forth so that people may know the power of intellect and organization. People will feel the miracle of divine power when the intellect is properly motivated.

"Justice should get its due respect. Moral values should receive proper recognition. All people should live together and share their gains equally. When

---

[2]There are unbelievable changes in the world. For example, one Communist government of Eastern Europe fell, the others toppled rapidly after it. I believe that the harmony now sweeping Europe, South Africa, and other countries flows from the efforts of Shree Ram Sharma.

these principles are absorbed into the souls of mankind, humanity will find proper direction. Bold new ventures will be planned and the harmony will ultimately emerge.

"If men will follow the two principles of atmavat sarvabhoteshu (everyone has the same soul--the unity of all souls) and vasudhaiva kutumbakam (the whole world is one family), they will recognize the evil in their lives and what they require to cast it out. Once a person determines to do something because it is right, nothing becomes too difficult.

"There is going to be one world, one language, one religion and one culture in the near future. The day is not far off when discrimination because of caste, class, sex, or money will come to an end: for humanity will see how we are shackled, and thinking persons will heroically set us free. The time is soon to come. We may anxiously look forward to it."

Sagacious Resolve For Era Creation

1. I consider piousness and devotion to duty to be the sacred obligations of human life.

2. I shall take care of my health by self-restraint and regularity of living, knowing that the body is the temple of God.

3. I shall always keep my mind pure, regarding it to be the point of convergence of vital forces.

4. In order to shield the mind from bad thoughts and harmful sentiments, I shall manage to keep up my studies and be in good company.

5. I shall consider myself to be an integral part of the society and shall accept my good in the welfare of all members of the society.

6. I shall not consider my own individual self - interest and happiness more important than collective interest and happiness of society.

7. I shall realize that virtues like citizenship, moral-righteousness, humility, good character, politeness, broad-mindedness, spirit of kinship, equality, and tolerance are the true wealth of mankind and shall always strive to promote these virtues in personal life.

8. I shall not neglect or remain indifferent towards the acts of meditation, study, self-control, and service.

9. I shall create an atmosphere of pleasantness, cleanliness, simplicity, and gentlemanliness all around.

10. I shall give due importance to discretion in relation to tradition.

11. I shall welcome failure when following the path of righteousness rather than success through sinful means.

12. I shall test the worthiness of a man not by his successes, qualifications, and prosperity but by his good thoughts and his benevolent acts.

13. My life will be spent in doing acts of benevolence and not in selfishness.

14. I shall regularly devote a part of my time, power, knowledge, diligence, and wealth for the holy propagation of noble activities in the world.

15. I shall not behave with others in a way in which I do not expect others to behave with me.

16. I shall accept earnings only from my own labour and through honest means.

17. I shall faithfully observe the moral duty of devotion to my husband or wife.

18. On the basis of confidence in the statement that "Man is the master of his own destiny" I believe that I shall obtain distinction and, help others to also excel in life. This will definitely result in a fundamental change in the epoch.

Our resolve for making a new epoch

shall certainly be fulfilled

Chapter 15

The Fourth and Final Direction

Written by Shree Ram Sharma Acharya and translated by Shree Satyanarayan Pandya.

A message was received as in the past, and I was summoned to the Himalayas for the fourth time for a week in 1984. How could there by delay in compliance with the instructions? Although physically I am engaged in doing the work entrusted to me, my mind has always remained in the inaccessible Himalayas with Gurudev who lives in the Himalayas but whose mind always hovers around me. His voice always echoes in my inner-self in the form of inspiration. He winds the key and my heart, my mind throbs and jumps like a pendulum.

The journey was as difficult as before. This time on account of my maturity, I was summoned in my astral body which had to appear again in three tests simultaneously. As before, I reached Gomukh and from there I was escorted to Tapovan. I never asked where Gurudev's astral body lives and what it does. I am only familiar with our meeting place, the velvety carpet. I picked up the flower known as Supreme Divine Lotus and placed it on the holy feet of Gurudev. This time also, after exchange of adorations, salutations and blessings, talks were resumed. Throughout the way, I was thinking that whenever I was called, I was asked to leave the old place. Probably this may happen this time also. I may be asked to leave Shanti-kunj and live in this Rushi hermitage and may be entrusted with some important work.

Gurudev expressed satisfaction on work done so far. I told him that everything was being done by him and its credit was being given to me. Having fully surrendered myself, it was for him to take whatever work he wished from me.

Gurudev said, "Whatever you were asked to do till now was local and ordinary which can be done by any senior person as was done in the past. All these works will now be done by your followers and you will have to take up more important responsibilities. These days the physical as well as subtle atmosphere has become so much poisonous that human dignity has been endangered. The future seems to be grim, dark and dreadful. To fight it out we will have to do indirectly all that which may be called singular and supernatural. The air surrounding the earth, its water and land have all become poisonous. Scientific advancement has made an unholy alliance with avarice and poison has been spread everywhere by mechanization, which means that the risk of informity, disease and untimely deaths is hovering on everybody's head. The risk of using atomic weapons by any inexperienced person is so great that by slightest violation everything can be reduced to ashes. Children are being born in abundance like weed and straw. What will they eat? Where will they live? All these calamities and horrors, coupled with poisonous atmosphere would turn this earth into a hell.

"Whosoever lives in this atmosphere indulges in unthinkable musing and misdeeds, resulting in immediate miseries. Distress appears to be at hand. This is the result of invisible pollution in the atmosphere. Persons living in such conditions will act like beast and devil. It pains me to see the people and this earth, which is the best creation of God, turning into hell. It is heading towards a great devastation. Huge mountains will have to be uplifted, the vast seas will have to be crossed to solve these problems, and for this you will have to take important steps.

"For this you will have to become five-fold and take up strategic positions. Like Kunti[3], you will have to create five Sons of God, deploy them on specific fronts, and assign them different tasks."

When he paused, I said, it was for big persons like him to think about and find out solution of the problems. So far as I was concerned I was his child, a puppet in his hands, and I was prepared to dance to his tune. I asked Gurudev to kindly direct me in what I had to do. Right from the performance of twenty-four Maha puruscharans of Gayatri to participation in the movement for Independence, from lifting the pen and writing, to the performance of huge yagna and building a huge organization, I had simply played the role of complying with his directions and guidance. I told him that I knew it very well whose power was working in all these accomplishments. How could I

---

[3]Kunti, wife of King Pandu, had five brave sons who fought for righteousness and won the greatest war Mahabharat in Dwaparyug.

therefore suggest or give advice? I told him, I will do whatever I was asked to do. Every drop of blood and every particle of my body as well as my inner consciousness, I said, was surrendered to him, to the universal mankind.

I was given necessary instructions and signs and was told, "You have to transform from one into five. You have to do five types of work in five different manners. Five birds can live on a tree. You have to transform into five. This is known as transforming the physical into the astral body. These five will be astral bodies because subtle power alone can discharge these extensive functions. You have to nourish these five astral bodies so long as they do not get matured and are able to work independently. This may take one year or more. When they become powerful enough, leave them to do their own work independently. When the time is ripe you will get rid of your visible physical body."

This was the guideline given by Gurudev. It was all explained what was to be done, how it was to be done. I am not permitted to disclose all these details. I am doing what I have been asked to do. In brief, it should be considered to be as follows:

(1) Purification of atmosphere, (2) Refinement on environment, 3) Building of a new era, (4) Cancellation conclusion of the great devastation, and (5) Creation and development of divine men.

Gurudev told me how these five types of work had to be done, how my single entity was to be transformed into five portions, and how the role was to be played. He said, "For this you will have to retire from worldly activities and wind up scattering of energy. This is transforming the physical body into the astral body."

Gurudev continued, "You will be told from time to time what has to be done. You will be protected from demonic assaults which will be committed to terminate your life in order to make this scheme unsuccessful. There may be repetition of the past attack at any time in the form of assault on righteous attendants. But I will extend protection in all such eventualities. Now go on entrusting your work to competent efficient attendants so that you may be free from all the responsibilities and worries of the work of this mission. The great change which is in my mind will be disclosed to you at the proper time. Premature disclosure of that strategy in such a critical time is bound to do harm."

This time I was not detained for a long time and there was no talk about charging my battery. Gurudev said, "My energy will always be with you in invisible form. Myself and the Rushis will always remain and work with you. You will never feel any dearth or deficiency of spiritual power. In fact it will increase five times."

I was given farewell. I returned back to Shanti-kunj. The transformation of my physical body into the astral bodies started on the day Lord Ram was born.

Chapter 16

Astral (Subtle) Body

Hindu literature relates many occasions when a Rushi or Saint appears in two places at once. Is this possible? Scientific investigators have concluded that this apparent miracle can only be explained by the astral, or "subtle", body, sometimes referred to as an "out of body experience" (O.B.E.).

On July 18, 1896, Mr. William McDonald was on trial. On April 15 of that year, the prosecution proclaimed, he had violently attacked several people in Manhattan, New York. The prosecutor produced four witnesses, one of whom was well-known throughout the city as a gentleman of impeccable character.

Impossible, countered the defense, for at that very moment, the same Mr. William McDonald lay in a coma in Brooklyn, five miles away, as a medium for the noted hypnotist Dr. Hawainar. Several thousand observers witnessed Mr. McDonald there with them.

The judge was caught in a web. That each group could have seen the same man at the same moment in two different places defied logic.

The defense called the well-known Dr. Hawainar to the stand.

"Do you know Mr. McDonald?" the court asked.

"Yes", Dr. Hawainar replied, "he is a very good medium and that day at 5:00 I was performing an experiment of my hypnosis on him."

"Is it possible", the judge asked, "for a person whom you have hypnotized before you to be in another place at the same time in a 'subtle' body?"

"Yes", Dr. Hawainar answered.

Still the judge was not satisfied. Could anyone cite any other incident in the history of criminal law similar to this?

Dr. Hawainar could. On September 21, 1774, on a Sunday morning, Father Alfonsar Ligori paced back and forth laboring over his sermon, in his small church. Suddenly he slipped, struck his head against a chair and fell unconscious.

Throughout the day, his doctor tried to revive him. Towards evening, Father Ligori came around.

Immediately Father Ligori asked for his most faithful disciple.

"Father!", the disciple asked, "are you all right?"

"Yes . . . ", Father Ligori replied. "I have just returned from Rome. I tried to poison the Pope."

Certain that Father Ligori had dreamed, his parishioners dismissed the remark until, some days later, an indictment arrived from Rome: Father Ligori stood accused of trying to poison the Pope! Relatives of the Pope claimed to have witnessed Father Ligori attempt to poison the Pope on the afternoon that he lay unconscious in his own church.

When Dr. Hawainar finished, the judge rubbed his chin. Was it possible for an unconscious man to commit an act of violence thousands of miles away? If so, was it possible to commit one while five miles away?

Both sides spoke truly, he decreed, but Mr. McDonald should go free, for the physical body cannot be punished for what the astral body has done.

The scholar J. Mulldon exhibited the separation of his astral body from his physical self many times. He described his experiences in his book, "The Projection of the Astral Body".

A soldier of the French Revolution was killed in hand to hand fighting. Although his head had been severed from his body, it continued to talk. This incident is documented in the files of the French Government, according to T. Rampa in his book, *You Forever*. Mr. Rampa believed the speech of the severed head to be the work of the soldier's astral body.

An accomplished master of yoga can separate his or her soul energy and consciousness from the body at will and then reconnect the two after months, or even years.

Saint Haridas consciously separated his soul energy from his body. His body was then buried in the ground and watched, night and day, by officers of the police of Emperor Ranjit Singh's government, and the British government. After six months, his body was exhumed and examined by both French and British doctors, who unanimously pronounced him dead. Yet, a few minutes later, Saint Haridas opened his eyes, regained control over his body, and lived therein for many years. Saint Haridas was a spiritual scientist who learned, in accord with true Cosmic Laws, to control the involuntary fictions that limit the uneducated. This entire incident is recorded in the published memoirs of the British governor of the time.

The astral body can separate from the physical body and reach any corner of the globe within seconds.

Since most of us cannot remember what occurs while we sleep, we are surprised by tales of out of body experiences.

In 1984, Guruji began his transformation of his one physical body into five astral bodies. Now mature, each one set in the direction determined by Guruji as he created it, these astral bodies act entirely on their own.

The first labors to purify the Earth's atmosphere. The second works to improve the environment. Shree Ram's third astral body strives to hasten the new era of harmony and enlightenment. His fourth does penance to avert the calamities scheduled to usher in that new era. The fifth works to create and develop divine men and women.

Shree Ram discusses his astral selves in his book, *My Will and Heritage* (published 1988), in the chapter entitled "Transformation of The Physical into Astral: SOOKSHMIKARAN". In Brief:

Historically, this time is a transition between eras. I have been instructed to stick to my guns and work hard these last twenty years. I have accomplished more in the 1980's than in the last 30 years. We prepared. We built energy. One can hardly describe the vigilance, the concentration, the resolute industriousness of these years. Little is visible to the naked eye; the rest remains concealed.

Twelve years remain in this transitional period. The wheel will turn with more speed, now, to attain

*the goal by 2000 A.D. In this, I will have to play the role
of a vulture and a squirrel.[4] In times of war, the
responsibilities of a commander and a cook are equally
important. At such times, nobody can disregard his
duties.*

*It will be necessary to attack on several fronts,
during this period. In war, the responsibilities of a
commander heighten; his thinking must become more
intense, more acute. He must consider how many
soldiers to deploy on a particular front; provide arms,
ammunition and rations; staff and equip hospitals;
dispose of the dead and dig trenches for the next front.
One slipped link in his chain turns his attack topsy-
turvy.*

*As I increase my activities, the greatest
limitation is that of the human body. It has finite
limits; I have an infinite task. How can all the work be
done?*

*The physical body may be abandoned and the
work accomplished by one or more astral bodies.*

*One restriction on the physical body is KARMA:
responsibility for one's actions remains linked to the
body. Any balance in one's account is carried forward
into the next rebirth. [Therefore our physical bodies
may have to work extra hard to make up for actions in
our past lives.]*

*Some saintly persons accomplish so much good
in relation to the meager physical necessities that they
draw to sustain life, that they draw physical illness*

---

[4]In ancient times, King Ram had to build a bridge
from India to Sri Lanka. A vulture carried stones to the site
for him, and a squirrel brought sand to use as "cement"
between the stones.

upon their final days so that they end their days "neutral" and so carry no karma into their next life.

In the astral state, all limitations fall away. The astral body, the sookshma, can discharge many responsibilities at the same time. Thoughts can be communicated without the barrier of language. This is the greatest convenience.

A man can walk barely three miles an hour. A person has only one tongue with which to speak. The astral body, however, can see, hear, and speak in many places at once. In an earlier age, the Lord Krishna appeared to dance with several ladies at once, and at his death observers saw him in many forms and several places at once. They merely glimpsed the potential of his astral body.

Not everyone reaches this level at death. Evil spirits and ghosts remain in astral form, but only on the crudest level. Perhaps they can make their simplest needs known to a few who knew them best.

Souls that reach the level of pitars, our deceased ancestors, function on a higher level. Their wisdom and maturity shows.

It requires great effort and divine assistance to empower the astral body. Developing an astral body is an important step in raising an ordinary person to the level of a divine person [siddha purush]. Along the way, the physical body begins to acquire divine powers, which the wisest use to help others. Yet the limitations of the physical remain, and accounts of supernatural achievements by "saints" should be viewed skeptically.

My current, ongoing transformation begins during this life and will continue even after abandoning the physical body. It requires great diligence, much penance, and the ability to channel a great effort into specific tasks. It is the next phase of the labor for divine power.

The next stage varies for each individual according to his current level of advancement and receptivity to spiritual guidance. No single curriculum works for everyone. An egg remains in its shell until it develops; once mature, the chick breaks its shell, begins to run and learns to fly. The transformation into the astral shares many similarities . . .

In addition, creating an astral self which shadows the physical body can be a great help. During this stage, one must avoid the temptation to misuse one's new power.

Most astral spirits have been described as hateful or moral midgets, perhaps because they died violent deaths and can only focus on revenge. At the same time, however, ancient scriptures describe persons of great devotion or accomplishment living in astral bodies. Some, who developed the capacity to work through their astral bodies, were known as devarshis (Godly Rushi). As spirits they could roam through space, offering guidance to devoted persons. Even today, travellers lost in the Himalayas tell of being guided back to the right path. There are stories of yogis appearing and disappearing in the caves that dot the hilltops. Similar stories surround the Lamas of Tibet. The Theosophical Society believes that a team of devarshis in the central Himalayas, whom they call the Invisible Helpers, works incessantly to bring universal peace.

Such devotees are advanced human beings, extraordinarily capable and thoroughly practiced in *helping their fellow man. Although they could fulfil any of our desires at any time, they respect the law of karma, which only God can modify. Still, as a physician rushes to help a patient, or a rich man a poorer, these saints on the astral plane rush to promote righteousness, whether requested or not. They can help reform a bad person or make a good one more successful.*

For example, the man I call "Gurudev," Swami Sarveshwarandanji, lives in the Himalayas. In his astral form, he lives where no human life could survive. He guides me from time to time. That does not mean that I have never had to struggle or have never failed. Rather, with his divine cooperation my morale has been higher and I have driven further than I could have alone. I could maintain my patience and my courage in times of difficulty.

This is not insignificant, and is all that one should ask from a helper, be he of flesh or divine. Some think of divine assistance as a magic wand--wave it and difficulties vanish. This is an illusion. Those who wait for miracles lose faith in a moment. We must discharge our responsibilities while looking for divine or astral assistance. Failures and challenges should be recognized as good teachers. We should step forward carefully, but with courage.

This is an extremely difficult time. People of the material world do what they can, but it will not be enough. Powerful astral bodies will need all their might to reform the spoiled among us. Their help will be necessary to solve collective problems of mankind and to strengthen those seeking to do righteous work.

Shree Ram's astral bodies began working on their own in 1987. They have set off the changes sweeping Eastern Europe. They have captured Premier Gorbachev's ear.

In a New Year's Day lecture, Mr. Gorbachev said that an "inner voice" had put his mind to change. We know whose voice. A few years ago, who among us would have expected to see the changes we have witnessed in Eastern Europe?

In South Africa, the winds of real change are stirring.

Indian national television recently ran a series called "The History of Ramayan," the equivalent of Tales from the Bible in a Western country. The director of the series and his son attended Shree Ram's Ashram as they began the film in the summer of 1988. How can we make the series more impressive, they asked, so that viewers will heed as well as watch? When it aired, between 10:00 and 11:00 each Sunday morning, the normally congested streets and bazaars, highways and bars of even so cosmopolitan a city as Bombay were deserted. Businesses closed completely.

In response, a second director just completed a series on the Mahabharat. A third has begun a series on the life of Rushi Visvamitra.

Observers report increased attendance at religious services. People's minds seem more attuned to religion.

This, too, is the work of Shree Ram's astral bodies. Look for more change as we approach the Era of Harmony.

Chapter 17

The Prediction
(Prophecy for Creation)

Divine Forces told Shree Ram to prophesy about the peace and happiness to come, so that those who listen will think of creation rather than destruction. By the year 2000, the world will not appear as it does today. Not only people's imaginations and feelings and thoughts and desires, but their social life, their work life, and their whole environment will change. All will appear new.

Those who dissipate their creativity on destruction will find that their brains have grown exhausted. People will start thinking in new directions: How can todays' materials be turned to the tasks of creation? Shree Ram says that those who work in weapons factories will have new jobs, making tools for surgeons or artists.

Accumulated pollution will close down huge factories and mills. Thus we shall bring water filth and pollution under control. In their stead, cottage industries will create the needs of the many before squandering their efforts on luxuries for the few.

Cities will fall apart and big villages will get rich. Gardens will blossom everywhere. Even deserts will turn green. New creativity will convert garbage into fertilizer, reducing pollution and eliminating filth.

Politics will improve. Assessment of a candidate's social record will select our leaders.

Acquiring the necessities of life will take less of our week; we will have time for physical maintenance and mental growth. Humanity will have time to begin developing essence of God.

Shree Ram Sharma Acharya tells it in his own words, in a free translation with necessary changes, entitled "My Prophecy is that there will not be Destruction but Creation", reprinted from his book, *My Will and Heritage*, translated by Shree Satyanarayan Pandya and published by Yug Nirman Yojna in Mathura, 1988.

All prominent persons have predicted, in their own way, that the years they faced were the most crucial and critical. The Bible contains many references to "seven times" when discussing the destruction of the world. This age is the Seventh Age. Islamic literature often refers to a great crisis that will take place in this, the Islamic Fourteenth Century. In the same vein, the Bhavishya Puran of the Hindus also predicts catastrophic conditions for this era. Similar prophecies have been made by Guru Granth Sahib of the Sikh religion. The famous poet Soordas foretold calamities during these days. There are similar narrations in the carvings of the pyramids of Egypt. Several Indian prophets and Saints have made similar predictions, from a spiritual as well as astrological, basis.

Soothsayers like Jeane Dixon, Professor Harar, Anderson, John Bavreie, Cheiro, Arthur Clark,

Nostradamus, Mother Shrimpton, Anadacharya and others who have considerable readership in Western countries, and whose predictions have often proven correct, have also foreseen horrible possibilities. In a conference of spiritualists from all over the world held sometime back in Korea, similar fears were raised. A conference of "futurologists", specialists in the science of foretelling the future of the world, convened in Toronto, Canada, stated that we are very close to very bad days. Those said to be experts in the science of Astronomy say that spots appearing on the Sun and the frequency of solar eclipses have harmful effects on people residing on Earth below. The appearance of Halley's Comet in the beginning of 1985 has been said to be harmful to the residents of Earth because of its poisonous gases.

Furthermore, common sense tells us that an indiscriminate increase in the world's population will eventually make food, water, even a place to live scarce; existing supplies of oil, coal and essential minerals would not last even fifty years. Radioactive fallout from past nuclear explosions will cause present and future generations to suffer diseases like cancer. Should nuclear war ever break out, not only man, but all other creatures. and all vegetation will be swept from the Earth. The imbalance of temperatures caused by our civilization is likely to create havoc as melting polar ice raises the water level. Even the opposite, a return of the ice-age, is being predicted. The sum and substance of all these prophecies is that some major upheaval will come. Thus, we can easily imagine the possibility of destruction before our reconstruction, of melting before moulding.

Both politicians and journalists worry about the world; never have they faced such potential crisis. Several peace organizations dedicate themselves to trying to devise ways to avoid total annihilation.

This state of emergency is not hidden from the Rushis, as they watch from their astral bodies. Their divine mission does not let them remain silent at this time. Rushis do not perform their acts of penance to attain heaven, liberation or divine power for themselves. Rushis assume responsibility for doing God's work and they remain fully committed to it. Fortunately, even secular persons can reach these levels by leading a spiritual life.

The Rushis have been extremely kind to me. Through their divine power, I have been able to perform 24 Mahapuruschcharans of Gayatri (a specific number of mantras performed, in the proscribed manner, in a specified period of time, performed for penance) for the welfare of mankind. The Rushis believe that clouds of crisis hover over our world; they want to help. I am one of their agents in the development of spiritual power.

The present phase in the process of transforming my physical body into my astral body takes the form of a kind of penance called savitri sadhana. This is not because of any individual fame or superiority of the individual chosen, but simply keeps the stumbling feet of humanity of firm ground. The Rushis have entrusted this burden to the shoulders of my five astral bodies, or helpers, just as the Lord Shree Ram and his brother, Laxman, once sat on the shoulders of a Hanuman, a devotee of this Lord Shree Ram of epic Ramayan. This is merely choosing a "medium", for how could a battle as huge as [the epic] Mahabharat war be fought with a single gandeev [legendary bow]. Even a man as strong as King Hiranyaksha[5] was torn to pieces battling Bhagwan Varaha [the fourth of the Ten Main Incarnations of the Divine Spirit]. Common sense would call it an impossible task, but God will fulfill His own will.

I have seen from my own experience that demonic forces shall not be allowed to succeed. Those who now pursue destruction shall either themselves be destroyed, or new people will be born who will overthrow them. Thus will the changeover be effected. India may play a prominent role in this new world peace.

Although most prominent thinkers prophesied annihilation, I emphatically aver that wrong will be redressed, that what seems topsy-turvy at present will soon be set right. Let me underscore the seriousness of that statement. The clouds of evil fostered by scientific advancement will be blown away by the violent current of the coming storm; darkness will be dispelled and light will appear. Only the mighty power of the Rushis makes this possible. In this, there may be some visible role [for me], but the rest will be all invisible.

Do not assume that the Will Power of even ordinary people has no effect: agents of destruction must yield to awakened public opinion. As this new majority swells, it will draw the minds of the uncommitted into its wake. People will commit their talents and skills to developing good rather than

---

[5]A very strong ruler who once conquered all of the Indian sub-continent.

destructive ends. Intelligence is a great power. It creates miracles whichever way it proceeds.

The problems are interrelated, whether they manifest as pollution, accumulation of military power, immorality and licentiousness, or "divine" calamities such as epidemic or famine. We will, therefore, find solutions in abundance once our new resolve manifests itself.

Two main powers make or mar an ideal world. One is the power of arms and money, and the other is the power of intellect and organization. Subdued by the power of arms and subverted by the lure of money, people in the past have been compelled to act against their wishes. This power is demonic. From now on, we must push divine power to the forefront so that humanity may bask in the positive power of intellect and organization. The world will witness the miracle of divine power properly harnessed.

Justice demands proper respect. Moral values deserve proper recognition. All mankind should live as one and share their gains equally. When the world earnestly adopts these principles, mankind will move in the right direction. New plans will materialize and our goal reached.

When we allow ourselves to be guided by the two great Hindu principles of The Equality of All Souls (atmavat sarvabhotesu) and The World as One Family (vasudhavia kutumbakam), we recognize evil for what it is and will find the strength to give it up. Fortunately, the power of man is unlimited; once a person resolves to do what is right, there is nothing s/he cannot do.

In the near future, we will enjoy one world, with one language, one religion and one culture. The day is not far off when discrimination because of caste, class, sex, or money will end. People will recognize what must be done and, guided by the right ideals, will accomplish this heroic task. The time is soon. We anxiously look forward to it.

Chapter 18

Two Words

The Almighty, Omnipotent, Supreme God is the same for all nations and all people, whether Hindu, Jew, Christian, Muslim, or Buddhist.

Jesus, Krishna, Ram, Buddha, Mohammed, they were all Sons of God in their time. They all lived in a time before world-wide publishing facilities, radio or TV. If they had access to such media in their times, they might have forged one religion on Earth. Predating the unifying influence of world-wide media, many religions exist side by side, each one trying to prove itself better than the others. However, in our time, we do have these modern communications "miracles".

All the political and religious leaders of the world should band together to form one religion for all mankind.

Some might say that this is not possible. Why not?

Witness the changes in Eastern Europe--did you expect to see those changes in your lifetime? Did you ever expect to witness democracy in Russia and racial progress in South Africa?

If there were only one religion and one language, then there could be brotherhood among nations. In the future, there shall be only one Religion and one language, as predicted by the prophets and scholars whose names I have mentioned before.

The changes that we now see in the world are the work of the Astral bodies of Shree Ram Sharma.

He has planned, he has labored, to bring harmony to the world. We, too, should help him by resolving those problems whose solutions lie within our power, by urging solutions upon our elected leaders, and by reciting the Gayatri mantra.

Countries with military power should restrain lesser countries who still wish to cause trouble for other nations. The Big Powers of the world should stop helping those who would make trouble for others. For example, America gives four times more aid to Pakistan than to India, although India is four times Pakistan's size and although Pakistan spends more of its U.S. aid stirring rebellion in India. Nations should insist that their aid money be invested in peace and not squandered in training for war.

Let us urge the powerful countries and businesses of the world to use their power to solve the problems of the world, without selfishness, and to bring Harmony around the globe, this wonderful creation of the Almighty, Omnipotent, Supreme God.

By promoting war, Russian ruined its own economy. Her people have to stand in line for hours for just a loaf of bread. Similarly, the race for armaments has left the United States with spiraling inflation.

Now the Messiah has come, and He wants to bring Harmony to the world. It is the duty of all of us who believe in religion, especially of our religious leaders and great scholars, to help in His plan.

In addition, to save the world, people should start reciting the Gayatri Mantra.

There are three systems of recitation.

The first is "mental recitation." In mental recitation, one can recite the Mantra anywhere at any time, in any condition. In the mental system, your tongue and lips should not make any movements, not even within your mouth.

In the "silent system" the tongue and lips do move, but a person sitting next to you would not hear any sound. This silent system should be used when you are sitting down for the *Sandhiya*. After bathing, you should dress in clean clothes, wearing nothing made from leather, and should sit facing east, sitting on a straw mat or cotton cloth so that the Divine Power does not pass through your body and into the ground, but remains in your body.

The Divine Power resembles electric current, and using such a mat acts like a ground wire for the current. Without it, the Power will not stay in your body.

This system of worship is called by the Hindu name *Sandhiya*. The *Sandhiya* should be performed between the early morning hours and 8 p.m. Ladies should not perform the *Sandhiya* or silent system for the five days following the onset of menstruation, but may use the mental system while performing normal tasks at any time.

Similarly, one should not perform the *Sandhiya* for 13 days following the death of a close relative.

The third system of Gayatri recitation is spoken loudly and accompanied by full ceremony.

The Consciousness of this New Age has been incarnating itself during this transitional period to annihilate any doubts in anyone's mind and to reestablish the superiority of righteousness. Gayatri is increasing in the present age in the form of Divine Superior Intelligence.

If you feel uncertain about changing your religion, you don't have to. You can recite the Gayatri Mantra with your God or whomever you believe in.

Sit facing east. When you recite the Gayatri mantra, imagine your God in divine, supreme light. As there is no shape to the Divine Light, it is easier to visualize the sun as the Divine Light. Picture this Omnipotent, Supreme God, or whomever you believe in, as the sun, throwing rays of divine, golden-yellow rays on you and your body. Allow yourself to be filled with it, filling your whole body with the Divine Light, as bright as the sun, destroying evil and adding virtue, righteousness and energy, transforming your individual self into the Divine Structure.

Is it necessary to have a guru? If you have one, it helps a lot. If you want to learn any subject, you usually go to a specialist.

Remember the example of actor Peter Sellers, cited earlier. He started reciting the Gayatri spell and suddenly he was saved. Why? Because the guru who gave the mantra to him knew that he would not recite it every day told him to recite it in emergencies. Was it pure coincidence that Peter Sellers needed the mantra so soon after learning it? I believe that his guru must have given Mr. Sellers some of his power so that when he recited it in time of difficulty, it worked like a bomb. Your guru can be your guide.

There are many instances of a guru helping his student. If you can't find a guru for the Mantra, just imagine one. The *Mahabharat* tells of Ekalaviya, who wanted to learn the science of archery. However the greatest teacher in his state, Dronacharya, refused to tutor him, for Ekalaviya had not been born to the kingly warrior caste. However, Ekalaviya made a clay statue of Guru Dronacharya, and the inspiration he received from his "guru" made him the best archer of his time. Even your God can be your guru.

Some people believe that you can have only one guru. Yet a teacher of English would not tutor you in mathematics. If you want to improve your ability to solve problems, you would seek out a mathematician. There is no harm in having more than one guru.

Even if you are presently reciting another mantra, you can start, simultaneously, to recite the Gayatri spell too.

The sages of the Himalayas are promised to help those who seriously want to help bring Harmony to the world by giving them direction. These serious students must perform their *Sandhiya* between the hour before sunrise and the hour after sunrise.

Shree Ram does not desire fame, nor even public claims that he is the Incarnation. Basing his arguments on specific prophecies of the Western world, and of the *Kalkipuran* and other ancient prophetic works, a noted author argued about ten years ago that Shree Ram Sharma Acharya is the Messenger of God, Messiah. When Shree Ram learned of this, he sent for the entire printing of the book and burned every copy.

"Why, Guruji?" his co-workers asked.

"If people of the world learn of this book," he explained patiently, "they will come to me in droves, and that will hinder the performance of God's work for which I am born."

We believe that the time is now ripe for people to learn of Shree Ram. Shree Ram Sharma Acharya works to uplift not only his own people but the entire world. He, with the help of his five astral (subtle) bodies, strives to change this era, the Kali Yug into the Sat Yug, the Era of Harmony.

No citizen of the world should feel hurt or slighted because the Messiah has been born in India and to the Vedic religion. It was the wish of the One Almighty, Omnipotent, Supreme God, which nobody can change.

OAM SHANTIHI, SHANTIHI, SHANTIHI.

Let there Be Peace, Peace, Peace!

UNEXPECTED

It was my wish to publish this book in presence of His Holiness Gurudev Shri Ram Sharma Acharya. Unfortunately he entered *mahasamadhi* (soul's final conscious exit from a yogi's body) in Hardwar, India, on June 2, 1990.